Quick Quality Check for Infant and Toddler Programs

Michelle Knoll
and Marion O'Brien

Redleaf Press
St. Paul

Published by: Redleaf Press
a division of Resources for Child Caring
450 N. Syndicate, Suite 5
St. Paul, MN 55104

Distributed by: Gryphon House
Mailing Address:
P.O. Box 207
Beltsville, MD 20704-0207

Library of Congress Cataloging-in-Publication Data

Knoll, Michelle, 1960–
    Quick quality check for infant and toddler programs / Michelle Knoll and
Marion O'Brien.
        p. cm.
    Includes bibliographical refrences.
    ISBN 1-929610-11-4
    1. Child care services—Evaluation. 2. Child care workers—Rating of. 3.
Infants—Care—Evaluation. 4. Toddlers—Care—Evaluation. 5. Day care
centers—Administration. I. O'Brien, Marion. II Title.

HQ778.5 .K64 2001
362.71'2—dc21
                                                                2001019994

To our families, Mark, Ben, and Kayla,
and John, Connor, Shay, and Lia,
with thanks for all of their support

Contents

Acknowledgments

We thank the dedicated teachers and directors in all the child care centers we have visited and observed over many years.

We are especially grateful to those who gave us valuable feedback on the Quick Quality Check items and procedures, as well as encouragement to publish Quick Quality Check: Gretchen Goodman with Sunnyside Infant/Toddler Program, Diana Irey with First United Methodist Church Daycare, Marcy Kull with Holy Name Early Childhood Development Center, Michelle Lausier with Bright Horizons, Alice Lietch with Kindercare, Patti McCulley with Parent-Child Learning Center, Shelly Platz with Stepping Stones, Renee Prusik with Kindercare, Patty Swartzel with Research Medical Center Child Development Center, Holly Turner with Children's Learning Center, Jay Weidenkeller with St. Joseph's Hospital Child Development Center, and Suzy Wunder with North Kansas City Hospital Child Care Center.

We also thank Alita Cooper and Don Bushell for their enthusiastic and valuable input on Quick Quality Check. Finally, we thank Jeanne Engelmann for her many helpful suggestions and Beth Wallace for her support and encouragement.

Introduction

As a busy child care center director, you may find it difficult to evaluate the quality and consistency of care your infant and toddler programs provide. Occasional checking may be possible, but time and other limitations can make consistent monitoring difficult. Let's face it—child care program directors are busy people.

Quick Quality Check is a practical tool that doesn't demand an unrealistic amount of time from program directors. Quick Quality Check requires a fifteen-minute observation during which the program director makes notes about fifteen aspects of child care that are organized into three categories. Each aspect of care requires only a "yes" or "no" answer. And, to avoid duplicating information that is routinely gathered to satisfy licensing requirements, Quick Quality Check measures standards of quality care not typically covered in licensing guidelines.

Quick Quality Check is most useful when completed periodically and accurately and when the results are shared with caregivers in an encouraging and positive way. By observing each classroom on a regular schedule, directors can be sure that their programs are operating according to the standards they expect.

Directors can use Quick Quality Check standards, along with licensing standards, to help train new or inexperienced caregivers. Caregivers familiar with the Quick Quality Check standards and who work to meet them will routinely provide high-quality care.

Quick Quality Check is best used as an overall index of the quality of care for children in a particular classroom, not to evaluate individual caregivers. Nevertheless, program directors can use the results of Quick Quality Check observations in staff meetings or in-service training sessions to help focus caregivers on quality indicators. Brainstorming with caregivers about each Quick Quality Check standard and ways to improve their classrooms' Quick Quality Check scores can encourage problem solving and sharing of effective caregiving practices among staff. And, perhaps of most benefit, Quick Quality Check provides an opportunity for directors to give positive feedback to caregivers when their classrooms score in the "Tip-top condition" range.

Quick Quality Check standards also are useful when talking with parents about child care. They are easy for parents to understand and support. Program directors can let parents know that they use Quick Quality Check regularly, thus giving them confidence that quality care is a priority. In the same way, program directors can use Quick Quality Check results in reporting to boards of directors or sponsoring agencies to show quality improvement or to demonstrate that a program is operating according to high quality standards.

Finally, as a program director, you can use Quick Quality Check to reassure yourself that what you think is happening in your infant and toddler classrooms actually is happening. Quick Quality Check provides a structured and systematic way for you to be certain that the children for whom you are responsible are receiving the care you want them to have.

Chapter 1: How to Use Quick Quality Check

Overview

Most children under the age of three in the United States spend considerable time in the care of someone other than their parents. Each year, more children are cared for in child care centers. Most organized care for infants and toddlers is of moderate quality: the programs are adequate but not excellent (Helburn et al. 1995; Kisker et al. 1991; NICHD 1996, 1999, 2000).

Because most child care centers must be licensed, they typically meet state health and safety standards. It's rare, however, for licensing agencies to set more than minimal standards for developmental and learning environments. How caregivers respond to and play with infants and toddlers is left up to each center and program director. Aspects of child care such as availability of toys, arrangement of space, and types of learning activities also are left to program directors and, sometimes, to caregivers themselves.

Caregivers who work with infants and toddlers tend to be the least educated of all child care workers (NICHD 1999). Despite the low pay and hard work, most caregivers report that they like their jobs and receive satisfaction from their work (Herrera and O'Brien, 2000). Most caregivers are dedicated to children and want to provide the best possible care for them. Too often, they simply don't have the knowledge or training to turn their good intentions into top-quality care. Caregivers may use practices modeled on the parenting they received or on their own school experiences.

Considerable information now exists about what high-quality child care programs look like (Helburn et al. 1995; Kisker et al. 1991; NICHD 1996, 1999). The most important dimensions of quality appear to be

- children's active participation with people and toys;
- caregivers' enjoyment of and enthusiastic involvement with children when they are happy and playful; and
- caregivers' sensitive attention to children when they are upset, fearful, hungry, or sleepy.

But professional agreement on the importance of these characteristics isn't enough to ensure uniformly high-quality care for infants and toddlers. This is partly because financial constraints make it difficult for child care centers to invest in higher salaries and better working conditions. Also, researchers have not effectively translated their findings into practical recommendations for caregivers. Exactly what can a young or inexperienced infant caregiver do to encourage "children's active participation with people and toys"? What are the components of "enthusiastic involvement with children" that make a difference to children's development? What does "sensitive attention to children" mean?

Given their extensive responsibilities, child care center directors often are unable to take the time to come up with practical ways to promote quality care in their classrooms. Although they themselves may have clear goals for the kind of care they want to provide, they don't have time to spend in training individual caregivers to meet these goals.

Quick Quality Check can help both directors and caregivers translate ideals into reality. By providing program directors with concrete, observable standards, Quick Quality Check sets an agenda for quality in child care. Similarly, caregivers who are aware of Quick Quality Check standards and who work toward ensuring that their classrooms meet each standard will provide high-quality care. Because the standards are specific and clearly defined, Quick Quality Check doesn't leave caregivers wondering what they can do to provide good care. Instead, both directors and caregivers can see where their classrooms are meeting quality standards and where changes are needed. (For more on ways to change the environment to improve quality, see page 31.)

With Quick Quality Check to help them, program directors can have confidence that the quality of care they want to maintain is provided routinely to the children in their care. Centers also can use Quick Quality Check to train staff, inform parents about quality indicators in child care, and document change in .their child care programs. Regulatory agencies wishing to move beyond basic health and safety standards will also find Quick Quality Check a practical and effective tool for indexing quality in child care.

What Is Quick Quality Check?

Quick Quality Check is a short and specific list of characteristics defining quality in child care centers. It is designed for use by center directors to become aware of and improve the quality of care in their infant and toddler classrooms. Quick Quality Check provides an easy way for program directors to take a fast but comprehensive look at their classrooms. It is a structured observation form and includes an explanation of each aspect of care. The Quick Quality Check guide also includes specific suggestions for changes in classrooms that will help caregivers meet the standards for quality care on which Quick Quality Check is based. Quick Quality Check can be used in a number of ways:

- ◆ in classroom evaluation,
- ◆ to make program improvements,
- ◆ in staff training,
- ◆ to provide parent information,
- ◆ in preparing information for meetings and reports, and
- ◆ as a guide to recent research findings on quality child care.

Quick Quality Check requires less time and effort from a program director than other ways of evaluating quality; it is a concise list of the most important standards of child care quality. Quick Quality Check can be used with little preparation, and the observation time needed is short. Other ways of assessing care in infant and toddler classrooms include lengthy manuals and training procedures, checklists with as many as eighty-four items, and observation times of two or more hours. By comparison, Quick Quality Check consists of a one-page checklist of fifteen standards and requires only a fifteen-minute observation.

The Quick Quality Check guide is unique in that it provides

◆ Information on each standard and why it is important for quality care, along with a guide to recent research findings that support the Quick Quality Check standards. (For more on what the research says about quality child care, see page 59.)

◆ Information on using Quick Quality Check to improve classroom quality (see page 31).

◆ A form for comparing results of observations made at different times of the day or on different days during a month (see page 9).

◆ Materials for training caregivers to learn and meet Quick Quality Check standards (see page 55).

In addition, Quick Quality Check measures aspects of quality care that licensing requirements typically don't cover, and so it does not duplicate other measures of quality.

How to Use Quick Quality Check

Quick Quality Check for Infants is designed for use in classrooms for children up to approximately eighteen months of age. Quick Quality Check for Toddlers is designed for use in classrooms for children from approximately fifteen to thirty months of age. If a classroom includes children across these two age ranges, both Quick Quality Checks should be used to ensure that all children are receiving quality care.

The following six steps will lead you through your first observation and help you perform each Quick Quality Check in a standard way:

1. **Know the classroom.**

Before using the Quick Quality Check form for observation, become familiar with the classroom you will observe. Spend ten or fifteen minutes there to absorb the "feel" of the classroom. Think about what prospective families see and feel when they enter the room. What is the experience of the children in this room? If you are well-acquainted with the classroom you will observe, you can skip this step.

2. **Select the form.**

Choose one of two Quick Quality Check forms, for either an infant or a toddler program, appropriate for the ages of the children in the classroom. Observe mixed-age classrooms using both forms.

3. **Understand the categories.**

Quick Quality Check standards are divided into three categories. For infants, the standards in the Play and Physical Care category are scored for each baby participating in those activities at the time of the observation; the Interactions with Caregivers category is based on all caregivers in the classroom at that time.

For toddlers, the standards in the Activities and Environment category apply to each child participating in the classroom activities during the observation (as opposed to being in the bathroom, for example); the Interactions with Caregivers category pertains to all caregivers in the room at the time of the observation.

4. Learn the standards.

Before using Quick Quality Check, read and study the descriptions of the standards used to check for quality. Refer to the standards and their definitions during the observation. It is important to score *only* what you actually see during the observation. Sometimes it will be tempting to check "yes" for a standard because you know it matches your philosophy for the classroom or what you know your caregivers have been trained to do. Unless you score what you see, however, you will not get a true picture of the quality of care. By observing carefully and scoring accurately, you will have a better idea of what is happening in your classrooms. You will also ensure that the final score is comparable to the quality scale provided at the bottom of the checklist. Your goal is not necessarily to get the top score every time, but to learn what the classroom experience is like for children at a particular moment. If the score isn't what you expected, then you can identify problem areas and address them.

5. Understand the scoring.

Each standard on Quick Quality Check receives a "yes" or "no" score, and one instance of a "no" leads to a final score of "no" for that standard. For example, if two babies are being bottle-fed during the observation and one is held while the other's bottle is propped, score that standard "no." If you follow this procedure, the total score will accurately reflect quality for that observation.

6. Observe.

Most Quick Quality Check observations should be done when a variety of activities are taking place in the room (as opposed to a time when most of the children are eating or are asleep, for example). Repeat Quick Quality Check observations at different times of day and on different days of the week in order to get a good idea of the quality of all activities in the classroom. Multiple observations will allow you to learn about a variety of aspects of the classroom, such as transitions and staff changes, and to identify specific areas that may need attention.

A Quick Quality Check observation can be completed in fifteen minutes. Some standards can be rated quickly, whereas others are scored after observing for the entire fifteen minutes. A score can be changed if, during the observation, you see something that you believe warrants a change.

Often program directors score Quick Quality Check standards with a "yes" when they did not actually see what the standard requires. This happens when directors are convinced the caregivers *usually* do what the standard describes but didn't do so this time because of special circumstances. For example, in the midst of an observation, a parent may come unexpectedly to pick up a child early, and this may disrupt the routine. In child care, however, unexpected and unpredictable things are always happening. Care must be maintained at a high quality level even when routines are interrupted.

Therefore, you should score "yes" only for those standards you see *at the time you are observing.* You may be surprised to find that what you thought was regular practice in a classroom isn't happening much of the time. By completing Quick Quality Checks accurately and frequently at different times of the day and week, you can get a true picture of the everyday quality of care children receive in your program.

If you complete several Quick Quality Check observations during a month, you can learn about variations in the classroom during different activities and when different caregivers are present. You may find that the Quick Quality Check scores are excellent at certain times of day and not as good at others. In toddler classrooms, it may be particularly important to do observations during mealtimes and transitions in addition to playtime. For these specific observations, you may want to use only the Interactions with Caregivers category.

Although Quick Quality Check is designed to give a picture of the quality of an entire classroom and not to evaluate individual caregivers, your observations may raise concerns about a particular caregiver. If that happens, Quick Quality Check can provide information on how to train that caregiver to make some positive changes. Quick Quality Check can also be used to encourage caregivers' continued progress or to compliment caregivers who already are doing excellent work.

If you use Quick Quality Check in a classroom several times and under a variety of conditions and the scores are nearly always the same, you can feel assured that you have an accurate indication of the typical quality of care in the classroom. If the Quick Quality Check scores are consistently high, you don't need to continue to do weekly observations in that classroom. Instead, you might bring out Quick Quality Check whenever there are changes in the classroom— new caregivers or new children, for example. It is also helpful to use Quick Quality Check regularly as a way of providing positive feedback to caregivers who are working hard and doing a great job.

To help you with your first Quick Quality Check observation, use the examples provided (see page 39 for infants and page 47 for toddlers).

Interpreting the Rating Scale

After you have completed your observation, you can find out how the classroom scores by using the rating scale at the bottom of the observation form.

First, count the number of standards that received "yes" scores. The highest number possible is fifteen. Then check the scale to find where your score falls.

The total score will provide you with information about the quality of your program and areas that could be improved:

14–15: "Tip-top condition."

A classroom with this rating needs only a monthly or fixed interval Quick Quality Check-up to ensure that it maintains high-quality care.

12–13: "Great potential."

Directors and caregivers could benefit from using the Quick Quality Check information to get a few new ideas on continuing to provide great care.

10–11: "Some action needed."

Directors and caregivers can see where a few problem areas exist and get ideas from Quick Quality Check about making improvements. Brainstorming with caregivers often helps them invest in making needed changes.

Less than 10: "Needs attention."

Directors and caregivers can go over the Quick Quality Check standards and their descriptions and work toward some changes that will make a big difference in the classroom.

(For suggestions on improving scores, see page 31.)

Involving Staff

Staff involvement in promoting quality standards using Quick Quality Check is critical. When caregivers are involved, Quick Quality Check is an opportunity for continual growth and improvement. You can use Quick Quality Check as a basis for staff training and as a focus for discussion of quality care at staff meetings. By sharing the Quick Quality Check process with your staff and informing them of the Quick Quality Check standards, you can clarify your expectations and standards of quality care.

Included in this guide are two handouts that you can copy and give to caregivers (see page 55). They explain the purpose of Quick Quality Check and briefly outline the standards. You can use these handouts when you introduce Quick Quality Check to classroom staff so they will be aware of the goals and expectations you have for them.

Initially, some caregivers may be uncomfortable with the idea of being watched while they do their jobs. It is helpful to explain Quick Quality Check's purpose, which isn't caregiver evaluation but a way to ensure that a classroom meets professional standards of quality care. Reviewing each standard with caregivers before using Quick Quality Check in their classrooms is an important step in recruiting their involvement and participation. Some caregivers may not agree that all the Quick Quality Check standards are important. This is an important discussion for you, as program director, to have with them.

The Quick Quality Check standards have been selected because they indicate characteristics that have been widely shown to be associated with high-quality care and positive outcomes for children. (For information about the reasons each standard was included, see page 59.) Your attitude of openness and acceptance when you discuss the reasons for the standards and encouragement of caregiver participation in deciding how best to meet them will go a long way toward developing a positive attitude toward Quick Quality Check.

Your approach to providing feedback about the results of Quick Quality Check also affects how caregivers view the process of working toward quality care. If results are positive and scores are high, you should give all caregivers credit for doing a good job. If scores are disappointing, you might want to downplay the total score and focus instead on working to improve the one standard that you think is most important.

For example, if you observe a toddler classroom several times and the total score is consistently ten or below, your most helpful response isn't to be critical of caregivers but to review each of the Quick Quality Check observations to identify the one or two standards that are consistently not met and that you consider very important. These will often fall in the Interactions with Caregivers category, as caregiver-child interactions typically are the most important determinants of quality care. Rather than giving caregivers a total score, which may seem to them like getting a low grade on a report card, talk to staff about their interactions with children and give them specific suggestions for improvement. Continue regular Quick Quality Checks to keep track of progress. When the standard you selected for improvement is consistently scored "yes," you can begin training on the next most important standard. What is crucial is regular improvement in the quality of care, not perfect Quick Quality Check scores.

In your efforts to improve quality in your classrooms, you may worry that if caregivers know you are observing them, they will behave differently than they do when you are not in the room. In general, however, people can't make major changes in the way they do things from one day to another. Especially in child care classrooms, where there are many competing demands on caregivers, it's extremely difficult for staff to change their usual way of responding to children.

If your casual observations at other times suggest to you that caregivers *are* behaving differently when they know you're doing a Quick Quality Check, then you know that caregivers not only understand and recognize quality standards but also are capable of providing high-quality care. This gives you an opportunity to discuss the situation with caregivers and to encourage that high level of performance throughout the day. For the most part, however, doing a Quick Quality Check allows you to see the level of quality that children in the classroom typically experience.

How the Quick Quality Check Standards Were Selected

The Quick Quality Check standards were chosen based on results of research studies of quality in child care, a review of other measures of quality, and the authors' own observations of infant and toddler classrooms. Most of the standards are tied to current research findings. In addition, all of the standards are supported by both the National Association for the Education of Young Children position statement on developmentally appropriate practice in early childhood programs (Bredekamp and Copple 1997) and the Child Development Competency standards for infant and toddler care (Wilson, Douville-Watson, and Watson 1995). (For more on the reasons each standard is important to quality child care, see page 59.)

Using the Quick Quality Check Tracking Form

The Quick Quality Check Tracking Form (see page 9) provides a way to compare Quick Quality Check scores from different observations and will help you interpret those scores.

Each time you complete a Quick Quality Check observation, fill in the tracking form. Keep a separate form for each classroom. Each column on the tracking form will provide information that will help you understand your Quick Quality Check scores. You can use the date category as an aid to planning your Quick Quality Check observations and to remind yourself when observations were done. By recording the day of the week and the time of day, you can look for score patterns based on day or time.

Listing the classroom staff present at the time of the observation allows for comparisons of score changes that may be related to staffing patterns. For example, there may be some times of day when there are more caregivers present, or you may have had substitute staff in the classroom on some days when observations were conducted.

Keeping a record of the activities occurring in the classroom at the time of the observation helps in checking to be sure you have observed a range of situations, including, for example, feeding time or transition from naps. This will provide information on the quality of care provided during particular activities. It is also helpful to record the number of children in the classroom during your observation to allow for comparisons across observations.

Quick Quality Check Tracking Form

Classroom:

Date of Observation	Day of Week	Time of Day	Caregivers Present	Activities Occurring	No. of Children	Quick Quality Check Score

Chapter 2: Quick Quality Check for Infants

Categories for Observation

Quick Quality Check for Infants involves observations in three categories: Play, Physical Care, and Interactions with Caregivers. These categories capture most of the experiences that children have in a child care classroom. Each of the standards within the three categories contributes to quality care as identified in research conducted in child care settings (see page 60). This chapter includes a brief description of the reasons the Quick Quality Check standards represent high-quality infant care.

Play

When not sleeping or receiving physical care, babies spend most of their time in play. It is through play that babies begin to learn about the world and understand that they can make things happen. Play is a positive learning experience for babies when they can choose among a variety of types of toys, have plenty of space and the freedom to explore that space actively, and are encouraged to be involved with other people as well as toys.

Different kinds of toys encourage different kinds of play. Some toys, such as soft dolls, fuzzy scarves, and bumpy balls, appeal to the sense of touch. Others, such as foam-filled blocks, shape sorters, and stacking rings, encourage constructive and functional skill building. Push and pull toys, large trucks, and foam climbers give children a chance to learn how their bodies move in space and to try out their developing physical skills. Babies need to have choices among all these kinds of toys and more so that they are exposed to many different learning experiences throughout the day.

Babies also need space in which to exercise their growing movement skills. When enough space is not available, caregivers tend to confine babies' movements in order to protect their safety. This can result in babies' spending long periods constrained in seats or swings. In addition, babies need space for the active exploration that is such an important part of learning, which takes place when they begin to crawl and walk.

The opportunity to explore and move arms and legs freely is very important for developing babies, so extensive use of infant seats and swings is *not* a hallmark of quality care. In many regions of the country, safety regulations prohibit the use of walkers and jump-up seats. Other kinds of seats may not be hazardous, but they limit babies' ability to move about and gain direct experience with toys and other people. Therefore, Quick Quality Check includes a standard that, when followed, helps to minimize the use of seats and swings by requiring that children spend only short periods—less than fifteen minutes at a stretch—confined in this way. Other uses of infant seats—such as for feeding or sleep—are not covered by the standards in the Play category.

Also important to babies' experiences in child care are the opportunities they have to watch and interact with other people—children *and* caregivers. The quality of relationships children develop in child care is important to their long-term social development. Frequent, positive interactions with other children and with caregivers build social skills and positive expectations for how other people will respond to the child. When babies are playing, the involvement of an interested and sensitive adult is crucial to learning and the development of new skills.

Physical Care

The standards in the Physical Care category cover feeding, diapering, and sleep. Because infants—especially young infants—require so much care, it's important for caregivers to consider these routines as learning activities and not just as boring tasks that must be finished as quickly as possible. For example, feeding times are intense experiences for many babies. The way caregivers respond to babies who are upset because they are hungry or who refuse to eat even though they *should* be hungry can influence how babies respond to food in later years.

Similarly, all babies must have their diapers changed frequently. Caregivers who use diapering times as opportunities for one-to-one interaction and affectionate exchanges are contributing to babies' development in a multitude of ways.

Sensitive care given at naptime is also an indication of quality care because it shows that caregivers recognize that the transition from being awake to going to sleep is difficult for many babies. Until they have gained enough experience to know that naps help them feel better later, babies frequently fight sleep, especially when interesting activities are going on around them. Once they have slept, however, babies need to return to active involvement in classroom learning activities and not stay in their cribs for long periods.

Interactions with Caregivers

How caregivers act with children is the key to quality child care. This is true for children of all ages, but it is perhaps most important for babies, who are not able to organize activities for themselves or, often, even move from one place to another independently. Babies depend almost entirely upon the adults around them.

Sensitive caregivers are aware when children are feeling upset, sad, or frustrated, and they are quick to step in to soothe, reassure, or help. Immediate and consistent attention to babies who are crying or behaving aggressively is important because babies are not yet able to regulate their emotions or control their behavior in the ways that older children and adults can. They need supportive adults around them.

It's equally important, however, that caregivers be responsive and sensitive to children who are contented and enjoying what they are doing. Babies like to share their successes and their good feelings, and to do so they need adults who are paying attention to what they are doing and who will celebrate and laugh with them. Thus, involved caregivers are alert to children's moods and respond in appropriate ways.

Caregivers in infant classrooms provide quality care when they talk to children a lot. The more language children hear, the more they learn. Being able to communicate with others, whether through words and gestures or just by facial expressions, is a major developmental task for babies and toddlers. By talking constantly about what they are doing and about what the children are doing, caregivers encourage children to communicate back.

One of the ways child care centers differ from most children's homes is that there are other children of a similar age in the classroom. Babies love to be with other babies, and they will watch other children's activities with much more enthusiasm and intensity than they watch adults. Babies also have a lot to learn about interacting with others, however, and their interest in one another can easily turn into unwelcome touching, pinching, and hair pulling. To make the presence of other children a good learning experience, caregivers need to promote positive interactions among children and to create shared experiences that help to develop early social competence.

Making Quick Quality Check Observations in Infant Classrooms

Before beginning a Quick Quality Check observation, you should be familiar with the general routines and organization of the classroom, be knowledgeable about the Quick Quality Check categories, and be familiar with the definitions of each Quick Quality Check quality standard. Look first at whether the classroom meets the standards in the Play category; as opportunities arise, you can also observe the standards for the Physical Care category. And, throughout your observation, you will be observing children's interactions with caregivers.

Play

When observing an infant classroom for the Quick Quality Check play standards, watch all the activities going on in the play area. Observe each standard separately—look for ten or fifteen seconds at each baby who is in the play area and decide whether that baby is receiving care that meets that standard. If babies are in the space designated for play but are sleeping or are being fed, don't include them in the observations for the Play category.

For example, begin your observation with the first standard: Does each child have a variety of toys available? Choose one baby in the play area and watch for ten to fifteen seconds. If a baby is on the floor with several toys within reach, that counts as a "yes" even if the baby isn't actually touching any of the toys. Similarly, babies who can crawl or walk do not have to be using the toys if they can reach them. A baby who is in a seat or swing and does not have any toys within reach would be scored as "no" even if there are toys on the floor nearby.

Then look at the next baby in the play area and again observe for ten to fifteen seconds, checking the availability of toys. When you have watched all the babies in the play area individually, you can score the item "yes" or "no." If all the babies in the play area had a variety of toys available, score the standard "yes." If even one baby did not have a variety of toys available, score the standard "no."

Next go to the second standard, watch each individual baby in the play area for ten to fifteen seconds, and score the item "yes" or "no." Continue in this way for each of the six items in the Play category. If babies move in or out of the play area during the time you are watching, simply score each standard for each baby who is in the play area at that moment. Don't include babies who are asleep or eating for the whole time you observe the Play standards. You do not have to watch every baby for every standard, but you should include every baby for whom that standard is appropriate at that time.

As you are watching the care each baby receives for each standard, it may be helpful to place a tally mark on the "yes" or "no" line for each baby. You can then place a check mark beside the "yes" or "no" line to show the final score for each item. One or more tallies on the "no" line would cause the item to be scored "no."

Physical Care

Your observation of the Physical Care standards can be done while you are watching babies and caregivers for the other Quick Quality Check categories. For example, if you are observing play, notice when a baby is taken to be fed, diapered, or put down for a nap and when babies awaken, and watch to see if the care provided fits the description for each of the Physical Care standards. Again, one instance of a "no" leads to the item being scored "no" overall. To observe these physical care routines, you may need to move around the room.

Unlike the other categories, the Physical Care category contains standards that you may leave blank if you don't observe them. For example, if no babies are being bottle-fed during your observation, leave standard 8 blank and count it as a "yes" in the total score. If you don't observe specific physical care standards during one Quick Quality Check, it is important to make another observation, on another day and at another time of day, in order to find out whether that standard is routinely met. By making frequent Quick Quality Checks and compiling your results across several observations, you'll get the most reliable and valid score for each classroom.

Interactions with Caregivers

When observing the Interactions with Caregivers category, use the same procedure as in the Play category, except that instead of watching each baby, you will watch each caregiver for a short time. You will be able to score a "yes" or "no" for some standards quickly, while others may require watching for the entire fifteen minutes.

Again, begin with the first standard: Is each caregiver responsive to the children's crying, gestures, or vocalizations? Watch each caregiver for about thirty seconds, noticing whether his or her actions match the description of quality care for this standard. When you notice a baby crying, gesturing, or vocalizing, watch the caregiver's responses. Using tally marks to indicate whether each caregiver fits the standard may help you track your observations so you can be sure that you have scored every caregiver on that standard. If any caregiver fits the description for a "no" for this standard, the final score for the item is "no." If you aren't sure if a particular caregiver should receive a "yes" or "no" after watching for a minute or so, move on to the next standard while keeping track of that caregiver's interactions with children. You can wait until the end of the fifteen-minute observation to score that caregiver's behavior.

Continue with the next standard, watching each caregiver and giving him or her a score at that time, if you can. If not, continue to watch caregivers until the end of the fifteen minutes and then score the standards for each caregiver. Include in your observation all caregivers who are scheduled to work in the room at that time, even if the caregiver is doing something other than caring for the babies. For example, if a caregiver is washing toys or straightening up, he or she should still be included in your scoring. This is important if you are to get an accurate view of the involvement of all caregivers with children on a typical day.

Descriptions of Standards

Play

1. **Does each child have a variety of toys available?**

    "Yes" means: The babies' play area contains toys that are available and appropriate for both mobile and nonmobile infants (unless the room contains only one age group). Toys are on the floor of the play area. Also, toys are available to the caregivers and to mobile infants on low shelves or in open containers. There are enough toys in the play area to provide all the babies with several choices. Nonmobile infants have toys available within reach and/or are given more than one toy during the observation. An infant mobile counts as one toy.

    "No" means: Few toys are available in the play area. There are not enough toys in the play area to provide all the babies with several choices. Or, nonmobile infants do not have more than one toy available for the entire observation.

2. **Does each child have an appropriate amount of space available to play or move?**

    "Yes" means: The floor play space is large enough to accommodate most of the babies in the room. Each baby has enough space to lie, roll, sit, and crawl in the play area without bumping into other babies or furniture. Toys and equipment do not restrict movement within the play space.

    "No" means: The floor play space isn't large enough to accommodate most of the babies at any one time, or toys, furniture, and/or equipment restricts the babies' movement within the space.

3. **Is each child who is placed in a swing, seat, or playpen removed within fifteen minutes?**

    "Yes" means: Baby swings, seats, playpens, bean bags, or any kind of equipment or furniture that prevents a baby from moving freely (even if the baby isn't yet mobile) are used for only short periods. (In some situations, babies may be in seats or swings for feeding or sleep. These babies would not be included in the observations for the Play category.)

    Scoring this standard does not require watching the clock, but simply noting whether any baby remains in a seat or swing for the entire observation. To score "yes," a baby who is in a seat, swing, or playpen at the time the observation begins must be removed at some time during the observation. Another baby may be put into a seat or swing, and as long as that baby is content, the standard is still scored "yes" because a full fifteen minutes has not elapsed. If a baby in a swing or seat shows any signs of distress, however, he or she must be removed promptly. A room that has no swings, seats, or playpens, or a room that has the equipment but no babies using it at the time of the observation, receives a "yes" for this standard.

"No" means: A baby remains in a swing, seat, or playpen for the entire fifteen-minute observation, or a baby who is showing signs of distress or restlessness isn't removed promptly.

4. Is each child offered experiences that promote fine and gross motor skills?

"Yes" means: Each baby in the play area has access to toys that provide practice in a variety of skills such as grasping, shaking, banging, pushing/pulling, and stacking. Each baby also has the opportunity to practice age-appropriate gross motor skills such as holding his or her head up, rolling over, pushing up, sitting, crawling, pulling up, and standing.

"No" means: One or more babies who are in the play area do not have access to toys that provide practice in fine and gross motor skills. Or, one or more babies who are in the play area do not have an opportunity to practice age-appropriate gross motor skills. This may occur when a baby is awake and being held by a caregiver throughout the entire observation with no toys available and no opportunity for motor activity.

5. Does each child have opportunities for interactions with other children?

"Yes" means: All babies in the play area are able to see the other playing babies. The babies are allowed to interact with, watch, and touch each other.

"No" means: One or more babies in the play area are not able to see the other babies. This may occur when a nonmobile baby is facing away from the other babies, or when the babies are prevented from interacting.

6. Does each child have opportunities for interactions with caregivers?

"Yes" means: One of the caregivers plays with or talks to each baby in the play area at some time during the observation.

"No" means: One or more babies in the play area are not played with or talked to by a caregiver during the observation. There may be no caregiver in the play area, caregivers may just walk through the play area, or the caregiver in the play area does not interact with one or more of the babies in the area.

Physical Care

7. Is each child who is being fed or diapered responded to and spoken to warmly by a caregiver?

"Yes" means: During feeding and diapering, the caregiver notices the babies' emotions and attempts to communicate. The caregiver tries to make the feeding or diapering enjoyable and adjusts his or her interactions to fit the babies' emotions and reactions.

"No" means: The caregiver does not notice the emotions or communication attempts of a baby who is being fed or diapered. Feeding or diapering is done mechanically, without much involvement. The caregiver may not talk to the baby or may respond to the baby in a perfunctory way.

8. **Is each child who is being bottle-fed held by a caregiver?**

"Yes" means: Every baby who is being bottle-fed is held at some point during the feeding.

"No" means: A baby is bottle-fed while in an infant seat or high chair or has the bottle propped for the entire feeding or entire observation.

9. **Is each child who is preparing for sleep rocked, patted, or held by a caregiver?**

"Yes" means: Each baby who is preparing for sleep is held or comforted by the caregiver until the baby appears calm and ready for sleep. The baby does not need to be put to sleep by being held or comforted but should receive individual care and affection before being placed in the crib.

"No" means: A baby who is preparing for sleep isn't held or comforted by the caregiver. The baby may be removed from play or placed in a crib abruptly without the caregiver preparing the baby for sleep.

10. **Is each child who is awake and ready to play removed from the crib promptly?**

"Yes" means: If a baby is crying, vocalizing, looking for caregivers, sitting up, or otherwise indicating he or she is ready to get up from a nap, a caregiver removes the baby from the crib promptly. Babies may be given time to wake up as long as they are content. No baby who has awakened is in a crib for the whole observation, even if apparently content.

"No" means: A baby isn't removed from the crib promptly when indicating that he or she is ready to get up. Or, a content baby who has awakened is in a crib for the whole observation and isn't removed from the crib before the fifteen-minute observation is over.

Interactions with Caregivers

11. **Is each caregiver responsive to the children's crying, gestures, or vocalizations?**

"Yes" means: Caregivers respond promptly and sensitively to a baby's crying by attempting to find the cause of the baby's distress and also by speaking warmly, comforting, holding, playing, or changing the baby's position. Caregivers also respond promptly and sensitively to the babies' gestures and vocalizations by noticing the babies' attempts to communicate, and interpreting and repeating the babies' vocalizations.

"No" means: A caregiver does not respond promptly and sensitively to a baby's crying. The caregiver may ignore the crying or may respond slowly or insensitively, for example, by shushing the baby. Or a caregiver doesn't respond promptly and sensitively to a baby's gestures and vocalizations. The baby's vocalizations aren't noticed or responded to.

12. **Is each caregiver frequently involved in positive interactions with the children?**

"Yes" means: Each caregiver is frequently involved in interactions with the babies in which the caregiver is warm, responsive, playful, animated, and affectionate. The majority of each caregiver's interactions with the babies are positive.

"No" means: One or more caregivers have few positive interactions with the babies, and/or the majority of one caregiver's interactions with the babies aren't positive. A caregiver is observed in any kind of a negative interaction with a

baby (for example, criticizing, scolding, using a harsh voice, rough handling, or physical punishment). Or, a caregiver shows apathy, boredom, or lack of animation in most interactions with the babies.

13. Does each caregiver stimulate the children's language by labeling objects, actions, or events?

"Yes" means: Each caregiver stimulates the baby's language either through direct labeling ("See, it's a ball!") or through descriptive conversation ("Katie is swinging"). Language stimulation can occur during play ("I'm going to get you!"), physical care routines ("Let's change your diaper"), or during any caregiver-child interaction ("Look. Suzy's here!"). Each caregiver is seen stimulating babies' language several times during the observation.

"No" means: One or more caregivers do not purposefully stimulate the babies' language several times during the observation. A caregiver may talk to the babies infrequently or may talk to them only when necessary or to control their behavior, without the purpose of stimulating their language development.

14. Does each caregiver encourage positive social interactions by helping children notice each other, use toys together, and touch one another gently?

"Yes" means: Each caregiver is observed participating in one or more positive exchanges between children. Positive exchanges occur when the caregiver positions babies so they can see or touch other babies, helps babies join a play group, helps babies take turns with or use toys together, demonstrates using gentle touches, encourages babies to be affectionate or comfort someone, responds enthusiastically when babies have positive interactions with each other, and talks positively about social skills and rules.

"No" means: One or more caregivers are never seen encouraging the babies' positive social interactions by participating in one or more positive exchanges between children.

15. Is each caregiver sensitive to the children's emotions and reactions?

"Yes" means: The caregivers adjust their interactions according to the babies' mood or temperament (quiet and gentle with a timid baby, more boisterous with an active baby), notice and talk about feelings and emotions ("You don't feel like doing that right now, do you?"), and are sensitive to the babies' reactions and expressions (noticing a baby's excitement, fear, or boredom, and adjusting activities and interactions accordingly).

"No" means: One or more caregivers behave insensitively to a baby's emotions or reactions (for example, ignoring a frightened child or dismissing a child's crying by saying, "That didn't hurt!"). Or, the babies' emotions and reactions are not noticed by a caregiver most of the time.

(For practice scenarios, see page 39.)

Quick Quality Check for Infants

Date:_____   Time:_____   Number of caregivers:____   Number of children in the room:____

Play

	Yes	No
1. Does each child have a variety of toys available?	❑	❑
2. Does each child have an appropriate amount of space available to play or move?	❑	❑
3. Is each child who is placed in a swing, seat, or playpen removed within fifteen minutes?	❑	❑
4. Is each child offered experiences that promote fine and gross motor skills?	❑	❑
5. Does each child have opportunities for interactions with other children?	❑	❑
6. Does each child have opportunities for interactions with caregivers?	❑	❑

Physical Care

7. Is each child who is being fed or diapered responded to and spoken to warmly by a caregiver?	❑	❑
8. Is each child who is being bottle-fed held by a caregiver?	❑	❑
9. Is each child who is preparing for sleep rocked, patted, or held by a caregiver?	❑	❑
10. Is each child who is awake and ready to play removed from the crib promptly?	❑	❑

Interactions with Caregivers

11. Is each caregiver responsive to the children's crying, gestures, or vocalizations?	❑	❑
12. Is each caregiver frequently involved in positive interactions with the children?	❑	❑
13. Does each caregiver stimulate the children's language by labeling objects, actions, or events?	❑	❑
14. Does each caregiver encourage positive social interactions by helping children notice each other, use toys together, and touch one another gently?	❑	❑
15. Is each caregiver sensitive to the children's emotions and reactions?	❑	❑

Total number "yes"_____

Total points:
14–15: Tip-top condition
12–13: Great potential
10–11: Some action needed
Less than 10: Needs attention

Chapter 3: Quick Quality Check for Toddlers

Categories for Observation

Quick Quality Check for Toddlers includes observations in three categories: Activities, Environment, and Interactions with Caregivers. Each of these categories contributes in many ways to the quality of care children receive. (For more on research into quality child care for toddlers, see page 62.) This section includes a brief description of the reasons the Quick Quality Check standards represent high-quality child care.

Activities

The play and learning activities that toddlers experience in child care are important to children's well-being and their later development in several ways. The Quick Quality Check standards in the Activities category reflect the importance of play. Children who are actively involved with toys and other people during the day are practicing useful skills in all developmental domains. Not only are they building fine and gross motor skills, but they are learning more subtle lessons about the benefits of focused attention, the rewards of persistence, and the joys of succeeding at a difficult task.

Children's development is enhanced when a child care classroom provides a variety of activities that are appropriate for the range of skills toddlers have. Toys and activities that encourage fine motor skill development, use of language, problem solving, and self-help are all needed, as are indoor and outdoor opportunities for large muscle movement and active play. Toddler interest and involvement in learning is highest when children are given choices among activities so they feel they have some independence. Thus, a toddler classroom should always provide alternative activities so that not all children are required to do the same thing. Toddlers also benefit from caregiver involvement in their play, especially when caregivers encourage more complex and cooperative play than toddlers are capable of on their own.

Toddler behavior is often troublesome. Toddlers do not yet understand or accept social rules, nor do they have the cognitive ability to view their actions from others' viewpoints. As a result, they grab toys from one another even when they already have toys of their own, and they hit, pinch, kick, bite, and push one another for no apparent reason. Often it is tempting for caregivers to try to keep toddlers separate in order to avoid negative behavior. Toddlers learn from experience, however, so frequent interactions with other children are important to their social development. Quality care for toddlers means encouraging interactions among children but guiding those interactions through careful attention and active caregiver involvement.

Environment

The environmental standards in Quick Quality Check are based on the toys and learning materials available to children and the amount and arrangement of space. Toys do not have to be the newest and most expensive, but a variety of kinds of toys is needed so that toddlers can experience many learning situations. Construction and building toys encourage manipulation of materials and play with a goal. Dolls and dress-up clothes give toddlers a chance to try out new roles and practice, in pretense, their own daily tasks. Books and pictures make it easy for caregivers to label common objects and properties of objects and give toddlers important preliteracy experience.

How toddlers' space is arranged affects what they do. The availability of a soft, cozy space, even if it is small, gives toddlers a refuge when they want to be alone or rest for a short while. Similarly, space for active movement is crucial for toddlers, who are more likely to run than walk in most situations. When space is inadequate, caregivers feel they must restrict toddlers' activity more than is healthy. Although access to outdoor playground space is also important, having enough space inside the classroom reduces the frustration of children *and* caregivers.

Interactions with Caregivers

Quality child care depends upon the quality of interactions caregivers have with children. In toddler classrooms, quality interactions are defined by active involvement of caregivers with children, sensitivity to children's sometimes rapidly shifting feelings, lots of talking with children, and positive and encouraging interactions rather than correction and criticism.

Toddlers are not yet able to structure and organize their own play. They are still learning how toys can be used, and their abilities to play cooperatively are extremely fragile. So it is important that toddler caregivers be directly involved with children during playtime. Effective caregivers suggest ways to play with toys that extend and enhance what the children are already doing. In addition, successful caregivers support the beginnings of social play by helping toddlers use toys together and recognize their shared experiences. Caregivers also need to be involved with toddlers during routine tasks such as mealtimes, diaper changes, and toilet training, and during transitions such as those to napping or outdoors. When adults provide structure and support for their activities, toddlers gradually learn to regulate their own behavior.

Sensitivity to children's individuality is another important component of quality toddler care. Toddlers are just learning who they are, and in the process they have to try out different personalities. This means that one day a toddler may be the most cheerful and pleasant child you have ever met, whereas the next day that same toddler is grumpy and difficult. Toddlers' moods can change rapidly and even a small upset can turn into a big deal. Caregivers help toddlers work through negative feelings by labeling the emotions toddlers display and by recognizing that children's feelings really matter. Caregivers who respond sensitively to toddlers are aware of children's feelings and their individual differences, and they accommodate their interaction style and expectations to the toddlers.

Typically, toddlers move from communicating with gestures and single words or parts of words to using complete sentences and vocabularies of hundreds of words. A critical part of this amazing change is hearing language spoken by people around them. In *Meaningful Differences,* Hart and Risley (1995) report that the amount of language children hear in their early years determines the quality and extent of their language development. Thus, the more caregivers talk to children, the more language toddlers will learn.

Toddlers have a lot to learn about getting along with others, and therefore their behavior is often difficult and troublesome. Effective caregivers recognize that toddlers' inappropriate, aggressive, or uncooperative behavior arises from their lack of knowledge and from their reactions to events occurring around them. Toddlers want to please adults; they simply don't know how. Quality interactions in a toddler classroom involve lots of positive comments, affectionate hugs and touches, and enthusiasm for what the children are doing right. When situations arise that are likely to create conflict, alert caregivers intervene *before* there is time for aggression or upset and redirect the children to more positive activity. When aggression does occur, successful caregivers don't focus on the negative but continue to give their attention to children's positive behavior. Nagging, criticizing, and punishment have no place in a toddler classroom.

Making Quick Quality Check Observations in Toddler Classrooms

Your observations of a toddler classroom will be most efficient if you are familiar with the classroom's general schedule and routines. Spend some time in the classroom, and make sure you are familiar with the categories of observation and the definitions of each standard before beginning Quick Quality Check. Look first at whether the classroom meets the standards in the Play category; as opportunities arise, you can also observe the standards for the Physical Care category. And, throughout your observation, you will be observing children's interactions with caregivers.

Activities

To begin a Quick Quality Check observation of toddler classroom activities, watch the toddlers at play. Observe each standard for approximately one minute, deciding if the activities going on in the room fit the description of quality care. It may be helpful to scan the room visually, watch each child for a few seconds, and decide if that child's experience fits the description of that standard. While you are watching, children may move in and out of the play space (to have a diaper changed, for example). Simply observe each standard for the children who are available to play at that time.

For example, begin your observation with the first standard: Do the children have opportunities to participate in teacher-involved activities or play? Spend one minute observing the children in the play area, noticing the activities available, and then decide if the standard has been met. Check "yes" or "no" to record your score. Go on to the other standards in the activities category, watch for approximately one minute for each, and score each standard "yes" or "no."

Environment

When observing a toddler classroom for the environment category, look at the toys and space available to the children at the time you are observing. Use the same procedure as for the activities category, scoring each standard "yes" or "no." According to the Quick Quality Check standards, children have access to materials if they can reach them without adult assistance *and* if they are permitted to play with those materials during the observation. Remember to score a "yes" only when the number or types of materials described in the standards are available at that moment in the classroom.

For example, you may be scoring the standard "Do the children have access to dramatic play materials?" If all the dress-up clothes have been taken out of the room for washing and there is only one other type of dramatic play material available, the standard would be scored "no," even though you may know that dress-up clothes usually are available. To find out what toddlers experience in their environment, you must score only what is present at the time of the observation.

Interactions with Caregivers

For the Interactions with Caregivers category, watch each caregiver in the class-room. You can take advantage of situations that come up while you are scoring the other categories. For example, while you are counting the available materials, you may notice two toddlers struggling over a toy. You can turn your attention to that situation to help you score some of the standards in the interactions category and then return to counting materials after the situation is resolved. You will be able to score a "yes" or "no" for some interaction standards quickly, while others may require watching for the full fifteen minutes before you can give a final score.

Start with the first standard in the category: Is each caregiver frequently involved in positive interactions with children? Watch each caregiver for about thirty seconds and notice whether he or she fits the description of quality care defined for this standard. Using a mark for each caregiver may be helpful to keep track of your observations. By tallying each caregiver, you can be sure you have observed each one, and you will know how many caregivers received "yes" scores and "no" scores.

Every caregiver must meet the standard in order to score a "yes," indicating that the standard is met in the classroom. If any caregiver fits the description for a "no" for this standard, the final score will be "no." If you aren't sure if a par-ticular caregiver should receive a "yes" or "no" after watching for a minute or so, move on to the next standard while continuing to keep track of that caregiver's interactions with the children. You can give that caregiver a score at the end of the fifteen-minute observation after watching more of his or her behavior.

Continue with the next standard, watching each caregiver for a short time. Give him or her a score at that time, if possible, or continue to watch caregivers until the end of the fifteen minutes and then decide on a score for each caregiver. Include in your observation all caregivers scheduled to work in the room at that time. Include a caregiver even if he or she is doing something other than caring for children, such as writing reports for children to take home. By observing at different times of day and on different days of the week, you will get an accurate idea of the quality and amount of caregiver interactions with children in the classroom on a typical day.

Descriptions of Standards

Activities

1. **Do the children have opportunities to participate in teacher-involved activities or play?**

   "Yes" means: At least one caregiver is directly involved with the children in the play area. The caregiver may be reading a book, helping with a project, playing with the children (with or without toys), or participating in any other activity with children at some point during the observation.

   "No" means: No caregivers are in the play area during the observation. Or, caregivers are in the play area but are simply watching the children and intervening when problems occur. Or, all the caregivers are busy with housekeeping or other tasks that do not involve them in the children's activities.

2. **Do the children have opportunities to participate in free play or independent activities?**

   "Yes" means: The children can choose what to do or play with. The children can play freely with toys and/or other children at some point during the observation.

   "No" means: During the entire observation, the children are expected to be involved in large- or small-group activities such as required centers, circle time, or a group art activity, and they aren't allowed to leave these groups to play freely. Or, there are no toys or activities available to the children.

3. **Does each child have opportunities to participate in social play and activities with other children?**

   "Yes" means: The children are allowed or encouraged to interact with other children. Interaction between children takes place during free play and during group activities.

   "No" means: The children are prevented from interacting during the entire observation and are expected to listen to the teacher or play individually.

4. **Does each child have opportunities for active physical play?**

   "Yes" means: The play area contains toys for active play such as a climber, tumbling mat, teeter-totter, slide, or rocking horse, and the children have access to these playthings at some point during the observation.

   "No" means: The play area doesn't contain toys for active physical play, or the children aren't allowed to use the toys during the observation.

5. **Does each child have opportunities to choose from several activities?**

   "Yes" means: During the observation, the children can choose from three or more activities. An activity is defined as a type of toy children can choose from during free play (such as manipulative toys, dramatic play materials, and books) or an activity occurring in the room that the children can choose from (such as listening to a story, playing independently, or participating in a group activity).

"No" means: There are fewer than three types of toys to choose from during free play or there are fewer than three types of activities occurring in the room to choose from. For example, the children may be required to participate in one or two specific activities during the observation and don't have any free-play time.

Environment

6. **Do the children have access to manipulative materials?**

Manipulative materials include construction toys, such as interlocking plastic or waffle blocks and wooden blocks; puzzles; stringing beads; activity boards; and other toys that promote fine motor development.

"Yes" means: During the observation, the children can play with manipulative materials and there are two or more types within their reach.

"No" means: The children aren't allowed to play with manipulative materials during the observation, or there is only one type of manipulative material available.

7. **Do the children have access to dramatic play materials?**

Dramatic play materials include kitchen toys, dolls, dress-up clothes, cars, planes, and other pretend-play toys.

"Yes" means: During the observation, the children can play with dramatic play materials and there are two or more types available within their reach.

"No" means: The children aren't allowed to play with dramatic play materials during the observation, or there is only one type available (for example, only dolls or only kitchen materials).

8. **Do the children have access to language materials?**

Language materials include books, battery-operated toys that "talk," picture cards, photo books featuring the children, and any toys such as games and puppets that are used to teach words.

"Yes" means: During the observation, the children can play with language materials and there are two or more types available to them within their reach. Reading a book aloud to children does not count unless children can handle the book and there is at least one other language material available to them.

"No" means: The children aren't allowed to play with language materials during the observation, or there is only one type of language material available.

9. **Do the children have access to a quiet, cozy, or private area for play or relaxation?**

"Yes" means: A reading corner, couch, soft chair, or pillow area is in the classroom and the children are allowed to use the area during the observation.

"No" means: There is no quiet, cozy, or private area in the classroom, or the children aren't allowed to use the area during the observation.

10. **Do the children have an appropriate amount of space available to play or move about?**

"Yes" means: The classroom play space is large enough to accommodate the children enrolled without crowding. The classroom is not so cluttered with furniture and/or toys that the children's play space or movements around the room are restricted.

"No" means: The classroom play space isn't large enough to prevent crowding, or the available space is cluttered with furniture and/or toys.

Interactions with Caregivers

11. Is each caregiver frequently involved in positive interactions with children?

"Yes" means: Each caregiver is frequently involved in positive interactions with the children in which the caregiver is warm, responsive, playful, animated, and affectionate. The majority of each caregiver's interactions with the children are positive.

"No" means: A caregiver has few interactions with the children and/or the majority of the interactions are not positive. Any caregiver who is observed in any kind of a negative interaction with a child (criticizing, scolding, using a harsh voice, rough handling, physical punishment) receives a "no" for this standard and the final score for the standard is "no." Even if a caregiver has more positive than negative interactions, the score is still "no." A caregiver also receives a "no" if he or she shows apathy, boredom, or lack of animation or interest in most interactions with the children.

12. Is each caregiver sensitive to the children's emotions and reactions?

"Yes" means: Each caregiver is sensitive to the children's emotions and reactions in the majority of interactions during the observation. The caregivers show sensitivity when they adjust their interactions according to the child's mood or temperament (quiet and gentle with a timid child, more boisterous with an active child), notice and talk about feelings and emotions ("I know you really want to play with that toy right now"), and are sensitive to the children's reactions and expressions (noticing a child's excitement, fear, or lack of involvement and adjusting activities or interactions accordingly).

"No" means: A caregiver is insensitive to the children's emotions and reactions as often as or more often than he or she is sensitive. Insensitive interactions include ignoring children's emotions and reactions, belittling their feelings ("That didn't hurt"), or scolding or reprimanding children without acknowledging their feelings or emotions.

13. Does each caregiver stimulate the children's language through activities and conversation?

"Yes" means: Each caregiver makes a deliberate attempt to stimulate the children's language throughout most of the observation (one or two attempts to stimulate language during the observation are not enough). Language stimulation activities include talking to the children about their routines and activities, listening to the children's speech and responding to gestures and vocalizations, repeating words and teaching new words, asking the children stimulating questions ("What does it look like to you?" or "Where is the red truck?" rather than "Do you have a book?"), reading, and playing games that involve language.

"No" means: A caregiver does little or no talking to the children during the observation. A caregiver doesn't respond to the children's attempts to communicate, or a caregiver uses talking mainly as a means to control the children's behavior rather than stimulating their language development.

14. Does each caregiver promote positive social development by helping children interact and cooperate?

"Yes" means: Caregivers encourage children to participate in group or joint activities, help children take turns or cooperate in using a toy or in an activity, encourage children to demonstrate actions such as comforting or helping someone, acknowledge children enthusiastically when they interact positively, and talk to children about social skills and rules in a positive and encouraging way. Caregivers promote positive social development when they are actively and positively involved with a group of two or more children by providing them with similar toys or participating in their play.

"No" means: The majority of a caregiver's interactions about social skills involve reprimanding children for not taking turns or demanding that children share or cooperate with each other without offering support for such cooperation. Or, a caregiver doesn't notice and take advantage of opportunities to promote social development.

15. Does each caregiver use positive guidance techniques such as redirection and positive reinforcement?

"Yes" means: All discipline and guidance that occurs during the observation is positive. Examples of positive guidance techniques include providing adequate resources for the children, explaining simple rules and routines in a positive way, and removing a child from an undesirable activity and redirecting him or her to another activity. Other examples include providing choices for appropriate actions, praising positive behavior, and briefly and calmly stating consequences for undesirable behavior.

"No" means: Any caregiver shows any instance of negative discipline during the observation, such as yelling, criticizing, rough handling, physical punishment, confinement, or inappropriate time-outs. Or, guidance is needed and a caregiver fails to provide adequate discipline or guidance during the observation.

(For practice scenarios, see page 47.)

Quick Quality Check for Toddlers

Date:_____   Time:_____   Number of caregivers:____   Number of children in the room:____

Activities

	Yes	No
1. Do the children have opportunities to participate in teacher-involved activities or play?...........❏		❏
2. Do the children have opportunities to participate in free play or independent activities? ....❏		❏
3. Does each child have opportunities to participate in social play and activities with other children? ....❏		❏
4. Does each child have opportunities for active physical play? ....❏		❏
5. Does each child have opportunities to choose from several activities? ....❏		❏

Environment

6. Do the children have access to manipulative materials? ....❏		❏
7. Do the children have access to dramatic play materials? ....❏		❏
8. Do the children have access to language materials? ....❏		❏
9. Do the children have access to a quiet, cozy, or private area for play or relaxation?...............❏		❏
10. Do the children have an appropriate amount of space available to play or move about?..........❏		❏

Interactions with Caregivers

11. Is each caregiver frequently involved in positive interactions with children?...........................❏		❏
12. Is each caregiver sensitive to the children's emotions and reactions?....................................❏		❏
13. Does each caregiver stimulate the children's language through activities and conversation? ....❏		❏
14. Does each caregiver promote positive social development by helping children interact and cooperate?...❏		❏
15. Does each caregiver use positive guidance techniques such as redirection and positive reinforcement? ....❏		❏

Total number "yes"_____

Total points:
14–15: Tip-top condition
12–13: Great potential
10–11: Some action needed
Less than 10: Needs attention

Chapter 4: Improving Classroom Quality with Quick Quality Check

After completing several Quick Quality Check observations at different times of day and on different days, you may find that a classroom doesn't meet some of the standards. In this chapter you will find some suggestions for making changes in the classroom to change the "no" scores to "yes" scores.

Usually, teaching staff also will have helpful and creative ideas for addressing the Quick Quality Check standards. Therefore, it is valuable to involve staff in discussions of quality care based on the standards on the Quick Quality Check forms.

These suggestions are guides to get you and your classroom staff thinking about how to improve quality. Not every suggestion will work in every classroom. Often, however, environmental changes—in space, assignment of staff responsibilities, or scheduling—can help raise the quality of care. Small changes in the classroom environment, which remove barriers to effective care, can sometimes result in big changes in caregivers' behavior.

Improving Infant Classrooms

If the classroom received a "no" on this standard:	Try these ideas:
1. Does each child have a variety of toys available?	◆ Move toys out of storage bins or boxes and off high shelves into the children's reach. ◆ Place low toy shelves around the play space so they are easy for caregivers and children to reach. ◆ Collect a supply of soft toys, scarves, and other fabrics that are easy for tiny babies to grasp and hold. ◆ Attach mirrors and activity boards to the walls near the floor where babies can see and touch them.
2. Does each child have an appropriate amount of space available to play or move?	◆ Clear unnecessary furniture and equipment from the babies' play space. ◆ Rearrange feeding, diapering, and nap space so an open area is available for play and exploration. ◆ Pick up toys frequently throughout the day, setting used toys aside to be washed and getting out new ones. ◆ Remove large toys that have lost their appeal and aren't being used.

If the classroom received a "no" on this standard:	Try these ideas:
3. Is each child who is placed in a swing, seat, or playpen removed within fifteen minutes?	◆ Minimize the number of swings and infant seats in the classroom. ◆ Establish a schedule of changing toys and play activities every fifteen minutes, and use this routine activity as a guide to when babies' positions should be changed. ◆ Divide responsibilities clearly among caregivers so each one has a particular task or area of the classroom (play, diapering) to supervise or particular children to care for. Sharing duties often means that no one feels responsible, and children's needs may be overlooked.
4. Is each child offered experiences that promote fine and gross motor skills?	◆ Make sure there are plenty of materials in the classroom that encourage children to reach, grasp, and manipulate them. ◆ Encourage caregivers to be on the same level with the children and to change positions frequently (at least every fifteen minutes) so children will move to be close to them. ◆ Provide some low shelves or other supports that are stable enough for children to pull themselves up with.
5. Does each child have opportunities for interaction with other children?	◆ Establish a routine that places only one caregiver in the play area with up to three or four babies at one time; assigning a specific play activity to this caregiver will encourage involvement with children and interaction among children. ◆ Encourage caregivers to sit on the floor while holding a small baby so the older children can see and (gently) touch the little one. ◆ When children begin to be able to pick up and eat small pieces of food on their own, have two or three share mealtimes.
6. Does each child have opportunities for interactions with caregivers?	◆ Make it clear that involvement with children is the primary job of caregivers whenever they are in the play area. ◆ Remove from the play space any equipment (such as a swing, crib, playpen, or high chair) that isolates children.
7. Is each child who is being fed or diapered responded to and spoken to warmly by a caregiver?	◆ Establish a schedule so that caregivers have specific times to feed babies and to take a turn at diapering. These tasks are more pleasant when shared, and with a schedule, caregivers can devote their full attention to the children they are caring for. ◆ Decorate the feeding and diapering areas with colorful pictures and mobiles to encourage children's and caregivers' involvement and interest while in these areas.
8. Is each child who is being bottle-fed held by a caregiver?	◆ Have a tentative schedule of feeding times posted in the classroom so that caregivers can prepare babies' bottles and feel less rushed during feedings. ◆ Arrange a work schedule that permits a caregiver who is responsible for feeding children to have no other responsibilities at that time (not doing laundry, supervising children's play, or answering the telephone, for example).

If the classroom received a "no" on this standard:	Try these ideas:
9. Is each child who is preparing for sleep rocked, patted, or held by a caregiver?	◆ Develop a short nap routine for each baby by asking family members what they do at home and sharing information about what is most relaxing for each baby. ◆ Encourage families to bring duplicates of babies' favorite sleep blankets or stuffed toys to the classroom, and use them only at naptime, letting babies hold and hug them for a few minutes before going to their beds.
10. Is each child who is awake and ready to play removed from the crib promptly?	◆ Arrange the nap area so children in cribs can be seen from other areas of the classroom. ◆ Establish a routine so that caregivers check on every baby at least every fifteen minutes (this can be combined with the toy or activity schedule mentioned in standard 3). ◆ Encourage caregivers to emphasize children's learning and exploration rather than the amount of time they sleep.
11. Is each caregiver responsive to the children's crying, gestures, or vocalizations?	◆ Arrange for caregivers to have occasional time away from the children when they can talk about each baby's personality and characteristics and share ideas for the best way to care for each one. ◆ Establish a system of clear and shared responsibility so caregivers have some time during the day when they can devote their attention just to babies, not to cleaning, record keeping, or ordering supplies. ◆ Observe individual caregivers with babies and talk with them later about the specifics of what you observed; emphasize the times they "connected" with a baby and offer gentle suggestions for areas where they might improve.
12. Is each caregiver frequently involved in positive interactions with the children?	◆ Review the daily tasks required of caregivers and make sure that their job descriptions emphasize involvement with children rather than other duties. ◆ Check the staffing pattern and be sure there are enough caregivers to accomplish all the tasks that must be done at each point during the day. ◆ Give caregivers a lot of personal support and thanks for their hard work. ◆ Observe individual caregivers with babies, and count the number of positive interactions they have. Later, report that count to the caregiver, in private, setting a goal for the number of interactions you expect to see per minute.
13. Does each caregiver stimulate the children's language by labeling objects, actions, or events?	◆ Emphasize to all caregivers the importance to babies of hearing a lot of language of all kinds: conversation, book reading, nursery rhymes, songs, stories, descriptions of everyday objects and events. ◆ Provide a small tape recorder with a clip-on microphone that a caregiver can carry around for a half-hour or so. Let the caregiver listen to the tape in private. This technique is even more helpful if you provide a guide to the amount and frequency of labeling and description you think there should be.

If the classroom received a "no" on this standard:	Try these ideas:
14. Does each caregiver encourage positive social interactions by helping children notice each other, use toys together, and touch one another gently?	◆ Help caregivers focus attention on children's interactions with one another by asking questions about the babies' social development. ◆ Observe caregivers when they are responsible for two or more babies. Later, talk with them privately about the specific ways they encouraged children to interact and make gentle suggestions for other approaches. ◆ When you talk with caregivers, emphasize the growing social competence of babies rather than their "difficult" behavior or protecting them from one another.
15. Is each caregiver sensitive to the children's emotions and reactions?	◆ When talking with caregivers about children, emphasize your observations of their feelings—whether they seemed sad or drowsy, cheerful or energetic, bored or scared. ◆ Encourage caregivers to record a brief description of each child's general emotional state when doing the daily health check or recording how much children ate. ◆ Observe caregivers when they are with babies, and keep track of their responses to children's sounds and facial expressions. Later, discuss what you observed privately with caregivers, emphasizing their successful responses and making gentle suggestions for change.

Improving Toddler Classrooms

If the classroom received a "no" on this standard:	Try these ideas:
1. Do the children have opportunities to participate in teacher-involved activities or play?	◆ Make it clear that involvement with children is the caregivers' primary job whenever they are in the play area. ◆ Develop or adopt a simple curriculum of play activities and assign specific activities to be conducted at certain times of day by specific teachers; one teacher per activity works best. ◆ Encourage caregivers to be on the same level with the children and to change positions and activities frequently (every fifteen or twenty minutes). ◆ Involve caregivers in the selection of toys and activities for the classroom; adults enjoy play more when the materials interest them. ◆ Establish a system of clear and shared responsibility so caregivers have some time during the day when they can devote all their attention just to children, not to cleaning, record keeping, or ordering supplies.
2. Do the children have opportunities to participate in free play or independent activities?	◆ Move toys out of storage bins or boxes and off of high shelves into the children's reach; keep them available even when teachers are leading more organized activities. ◆ Place low toy shelves around the play space so they are easy for children to reach. ◆ Keep toddler favorites—dolls and blankets, wheel toys, small baskets with handles—available all the time for holding, pushing, and carrying. ◆ Talk with caregivers about ways to divide responsibility in the play space (for example, by having one caregiver supervise one end of the area and a second the other end) so they can be involved in play activities and at the same time supervise children at free play.
3. Does each child have opportunities to participate in social play and activities with other children?	◆ Emphasize to caregivers the growing social competence of toddlers and their need to practice by doing things together. ◆ Point out skills and activities that toddlers have learned from watching and imitating one another. ◆ Remove from the play space any equipment (such as swings, cribs, playpens, and high chairs) that isolates children.
4. Does each child have opportunities for active physical play?	◆ Examine the classroom environment from a toddler's point of view, and add equipment or clear space so that the most active of the group can always find a satisfying place to play. ◆ Consider moving some outdoor play equipment indoors. ◆ Provide more than one of each kind of several different wheeled toys for riding, pushing, and pulling; keep them available all day. ◆ Place a large, thick (at least 3-inch) plastic-covered foam mat on the floor near a set of toy shelves or cabinets. Use it as a base for building with blocks and other manipulatives. Children also practice their balance by stepping onto the mat.

If the classroom received a "no" on this standard:	Try these ideas:
5. Does each child have opportunities to choose from several activities?	◆ Encourage caregivers to recognize that toddlers are learning from everything they do, and they don't have to sit and listen to adults or participate in a group activity to be learning. ◆ Emphasize to caregivers that toddlers are most cooperative when they are not pushed into doing things but given choices. ◆ Post an uncomplicated schedule of activities that reminds caregivers to pick up toys not in use and replace them with clean and interesting objects frequently during the day.
6. Do the children have access to manipulative materials?	◆ Make sure there are plenty of materials in the classroom that encourage children to reach, grasp, and manipulate them. ◆ Encourage caregivers to make two different manipulative materials available at the same time (soft blocks and airplanes, plastic interlocking blocks and wooden blocks); teachers will be amazed at toddlers' creativity. ◆ Keep manipulative materials such as activity boards and telephones available on play shelves all the time.
7. Do the children have access to dramatic play materials?	◆ Make sure there are plenty of "real" objects (pots, pans, wooden spoons, purses, and shoes) as well as child-size replicas of real objects (tools, hats, stethoscopes, shopping carts, and cash registers) in the classroom. ◆ Store dolls and blankets where children can always get to them; have twice as many dolls as children in the classroom.
8. Do the children have access to language materials?	◆ Make sure there are plenty of toys in the classroom that encourage caregivers and children to talk to each other. ◆ Invest in books, and enlist some volunteers to make books and picture cards by laminating magazine pictures. ◆ Decorate the walls with laminated posters and pictures that have lots of objects that can be pointed to and labeled; put the wall decorations at toddler-eye level.
9. Do the children have access to a quiet, cozy, or private area for play or relaxation?	◆ Examine the room arrangement for a corner or nook that can become a rest area. Equip it with washable pillows, plastic-covered foam shapes, and/or bean bag chairs. ◆ Protect a small area by encircling it with low shelves that are easy for adults to see over but safe and secure for toddlers. ◆ Make the transition into naptime by developing a short, individual nap routine that makes use of the quiet space.
10. Do the children have an appropriate amount of space available to play or move about?	◆ Clear unnecessary furniture and equipment from the play space. Toddlers prefer sitting on the floor when they are still and are in motion the rest of the time, so tables and chairs aren't needed. ◆ Rearrange the space used for meals and diapering so most of the classroom space is available for play and exploration. ◆ Remind caregivers to pick up toys frequently, set used toys aside to be washed, and put out new ones. ◆ Remove from the play area large toys that have lost their appeal and aren't being used; bring them back next month.

If the classroom received a "no" on this standard:	Try these ideas:
11. Is each caregiver frequently involved in positive interactions with children?	◆ Review the daily tasks required of caregivers and make sure that their job descriptions emphasize involvement with children rather than other duties. ◆ Check the staffing pattern and be sure there are enough caregivers to accomplish all the tasks that must be done at each point during the day. ◆ Establish a schedule for routine caregiving tasks so that caregivers have specific times to set up for meals and to take a turn at diapering. When caregivers have defined responsibilities, they can devote their full attention to the children they are caring for. ◆ Give caregivers a lot of personal support and thanks for their hard work. ◆ Observe individual caregivers with children and count the number of positive interactions they have. Later, report that count to the caregiver, in private, setting a goal for the number of interactions you expect to see per minute.
12. Is each caregiver sensitive to the children's emotions and reactions?	◆ When talking with caregivers about children, emphasize your observations of the children's feelings—whether they seemed sad or drowsy, cheerful or energetic, bored or scared. ◆ Encourage caregivers to record a brief description of each child's general emotional state when doing the daily health check or at some other time during the day. ◆ Arrange for caregivers to have an occasional time away from the children when they can talk about each toddler's personality and characteristics and share ideas for the best way to respond to each one. ◆ Observe caregivers when they are with children, and keep track of how they react to children's feelings, especially to displays of anger or crying. Later, discuss what you observed, in private, with caregivers to emphasize times they were sensitive and make gentle suggestions for other approaches they might use.
13. Does each caregiver stimulate the children's language through activities and conversation?	◆ Emphasize to all caregivers the importance to young children of hearing a lot of language of all kinds: conversation, book reading, nursery rhymes, songs, stories, descriptions of everyday objects and events. ◆ Have plenty of books available and replace them as needed. ◆ Provide a small tape recorder with a clip-on microphone that a caregiver can carry around for a half-hour or so. Let the caregiver listen to the tape in private. This technique is even more helpful if you provide a guide to the kind of talking you wish to encourage (positive comments, descriptions, and open-ended questions, rather than criticisms, commands, or yes-no questions). ◆ Observe caregivers when they are with children, and keep track of their responses to children's efforts to communicate. Later, discuss what you observed, in private, with caregivers, to emphasize their successful responses and make gentle suggestions for change.

If the classroom received a "no" on this standard:	Try these ideas:
14. Does each caregiver promote positive social development by helping children interact and cooperate?	◆ Help caregivers focus attention on children's interactions with one another by asking questions about the toddlers' social development. ◆ Observe caregivers while they are involved in play with the toddlers. Later, talk with them privately about the specific ways they encouraged children to interact, and make gentle suggestions of additional ideas they might try. ◆ When you talk with caregivers, emphasize the growing social competence of toddlers rather than their "difficult" behavior or protecting them from one another.
15. Does each caregiver use positive guidance techniques such as redirection and positive reinforcement?	◆ Develop a written policy that specifies the "rules" children are expected to learn, and emphasizes the learning process for toddlers. ◆ In the written policy, describe, step by step, how and when to use each of the positive guidance techniques recommended to help toddlers learn social rules. ◆ In the written policy, emphasize the importance of frequent positive interactions between caregivers and children and of caregiver involvement in children's activities. ◆ Review the policy carefully with every new caregiver and with all caregivers regularly at staff meetings or other occasions. ◆ Observe caregivers as they handle challenging situations. Later, talk with them, in private, about what they did, how effective it was in helping the toddler learn social rules, and alternative ways of handling situations.

Appendix 1: Infant Quick Quality Check Example

The following scenario will help you learn to use Quick Quality Check in an infant classroom. It describes activities and interactions that may be seen during Quick Quality Check observations. The scenarios are organized by category so you can practice scoring each quality standard. (For a description of how to score each standard, see page 15.)

Infant Classroom Example

On the day of the observation, there are six babies and two caregivers in this infant room. At the start of the observation, two babies (Alex and Benjamin) are sleeping in their cribs at the end of the room, one caregiver (Mandy) is diapering a baby (Kayla) at the changing table, and the other caregiver (Lia) is sitting on the floor in the play area with three babies (Jeremy, Katie, and Connor).

Play

1. **Does each child have a variety of toys available?**

    Jeremy and Katie are sitting on the floor while Connor, a three-month-old, is in an infant seat. Jeremy is pulling several toys off the toy shelf. Katie is sitting next to the caregiver (Lia) and is looking at some board books. Stuffed animals and a few rattles are scattered on the floor within reach of Jeremy and Katie. Connor is watching and listening to the play activities while lying in his chair. During the fifteen-minute observation, Lia talks to him a few times, but doesn't give or show him a toy. The babies who are sleeping don't have any toys in their cribs.
    Yes_____ No_____

2. **Does each child have an appropriate amount of space available to play or move?**

    As Jeremy pulls toys off the shelf, Lia puts some of them back to keep the floor space from becoming too cluttered. Katie crawls over to a play mat and lays down on it. The three babies in the play area don't seem to be crowded by lack of space or a cluttered floor.
    Yes_____ No_____

3. **Is each child who is placed in a swing, seat, or playpen removed within fifteen minutes?**

    Connor is in the infant seat throughout the observation. At one point, he begins to fuss a little, and when Lia leans over and talks to him, he quiets down. He seems content throughout the rest of the observation.
    Yes_____ No_____

4. Is each child offered experiences that promote fine and gross motor skills?

Jeremy pulls several stuffed animals off the shelf in the play area. Several other toys have been put away on the shelves. Jeremy pulls up to try to reach the musical toys that are on a higher shelf but he can't reach them, and Lia doesn't get them down for him. She suggests that he play with the plastic rattles that are on the floor. Katie entertains herself by rolling around on the play mat. Connor continues to lie in his chair.

Yes_____ No_____

5. Does each child have opportunities for interactions with other children?

Jeremy and Katie are both crawling around in the play area. They don't interact with each other during the observation. Connor watches Jeremy pull toys off the shelf while he lies in his infant seat.

Yes_____ No_____

6. Does each child have opportunities for interactions with caregivers?

During the observation, Lia talks to Connor on a couple of occasions when he becomes fussy, and she talks to Jeremy about which toys he is playing with. Katie spends most of her time playing on the play mat a few feet away from Lia, and Lia doesn't talk to her during the observation.

Yes_____ No_____

Physical Care

7. Is each child who is being fed or diapered responded to and spoken to warmly by a caregiver?

As Mandy finishes diapering ten-month-old Kayla, she notices Kayla looking at a mobile hanging above the changing table. She says, "Oh, you see the pretty fish, don't you?" She holds Kayla up on the table for a moment so she can see the mobile better and talks to her about the different colors of fish. After sitting Kayla down in the play area, Mandy puts Katie into a high chair and begins to feed her lunch. Mandy talks to Katie about what she is eating today and laughs when Katie squeals her approval.

Yes_____ No_____

8. Is each child who is being bottle-fed held by a caregiver?

Katie is fed baby food while sitting in a high chair. No other babies are fed during the observation.

Yes_____ No_____

9. Is each child who is preparing for sleep rocked, patted, or held by a caregiver?

Lia notices that Jeremy is becoming fussy and acting sleepy. She picks him up and says, "Are you ready for a nap?" and begins to gently sway back and forth for a few minutes. She slowly begins to walk with him toward his crib at the end of the room, while humming a song. Lia lays Jeremy gently in his crib, pats him for a minute or so, and heads back to the play area. Jeremy immediately begins to cry and sits up in the crib.

Yes_____ No_____

10. Is each child who is awake and ready to play removed from the crib promptly?

Jeremy pulls up and stands in his crib, continuing to cry. After a couple of minutes, Lia goes to him, helps him lie down again, and pats and sings to him for a minute or so. Meanwhile, Benjamin, who is in the next crib, has awakened and is lifting his head and fussing. When Jeremy has quieted, Lia goes back to the play area and sits down to play with the other babies. During the remainder of the observation, Benjamin's fussing continues and intensifies. Lia is busy helping Kayla get into a play saucer and is talking to Mandy about how much Katie should eat for lunch.

Yes_____ No_____

Interactions with Caregivers

11. Is each caregiver responsive to the children's crying, gestures, or vocalizations?

While Lia is getting Kayla settled in the play saucer, Connor is cooing quietly and waving his arms and legs while intently looking at the toys on the floor. Benjamin is still crying in his crib. Mandy continues to talk animatedly to Katie while she feeds her. Lia continues to talk with Mandy and sits back on the floor next to Connor, but doesn't interact with him during the rest of the observation.

Yes_____ No_____

12. Is each caregiver frequently involved in positive interactions with the children?

Consider all of the information in the scenarios already described.

Yes_____ No_____

13. Does each caregiver stimulate the children's language by labeling objects, actions, or events?

While Mandy was diapering Kayla, she talked to her about the fish mobile and labeled the colors of the fish for her. She also named the food Katie was eating for lunch and talked to her throughout her feeding time. When Connor began to fuss while sitting in the infant seat, Lia leaned over him and said, "Quiet now, you're okay." She also said, "Why don't you play with those?" to Jeremy when he wanted new toys. She also asked Jeremy if he was tired when he began to fuss.

Yes_____ No_____

14. Does each caregiver encourage positive social interactions by helping children notice each other, use toys together, and touch one another gently?

Lia moved Connor's seat so he could watch Jeremy as he pulled toys off the toy shelf. When Mandy finished diapering Kayla, she took her to the play area and sat her next to Jeremy, handed her one of the stuffed animals Jeremy had been playing with, and said, "Jeremy has a bunny. Here's a doggy for you." Neither of the caregivers talked to the babies about sharing toys or playing together nicely.

Yes_____ No_____

15. Is each caregiver sensitive to the children's emotions and reactions?

Consider all of the information in the scenarios already described.

Yes_____ No_____

Scoring

Play

1. Does each child have a variety of toys available?

No. While a variety of toys were available on the shelf and the floor where Jeremy and Katie could reach them, the nonmobile baby, Connor, wasn't handed or shown any toys during the observation. This category only applies to babies who are in the play area of the classroom, so the availability of toys to babies who are doing other things, like sleeping, isn't considered.

2. Does each child have an appropriate amount of space available to play or move?

Yes. The caregiver made an effort to keep the play space from becoming too cluttered with toys. The space is big enough that the mobile babies had room to crawl around.

3. Is each child who is placed in a swing, seat, or playpen removed within fifteen minutes?

No. Connor was in the infant seat when the observation began, and he wasn't removed during the observation. In addition, Connor showed signs of distress while he was in the seat, at which point he should have been removed promptly.

4. Is each child offered experiences that promote fine and gross motor skills?

No. In this scenario, Jeremy and Katie did have opportunities to practice age-appropriate gross motor skills by crawling, pulling-up, and rolling, but they didn't have access to toys that provide a variety of fine and gross motor skills. The only toys available during the observation were stuffed animals, books, and simple rattles. In addition, Connor was in the infant seat during the entire observation, with no toys available to him and no opportunity to get out of the seat to practice gross motor skills.

5. Does each child have opportunities for interactions with other children?

Yes. The three babies who were in the play area were able to see each other or interact if they wanted to. Connor was positioned in his seat so he could see the other babies, and the crawling babies were allowed to play in the same area. Lia didn't prevent the babies from interacting with each other.

6. Does each child have opportunities for interactions with caregivers?

No. Lia talked briefly to Connor and Jeremy, but she didn't talk to or play with Katie during the observation.

Physical Care

7. Is each child who is being fed or diapered responded to and spoken to warmly by a caregiver?

Yes. Both babies who were being fed or diapered were responded to and spoken to warmly by their caregivers. Even though only two babies were observed in diapering or feeding activities, observing caregivers' responses during activities that were seen during the fifteen-minute observation is enough to score this standard.

8. **Is each child who is being bottle-fed held by a caregiver?**

    Yes. No babies were bottle-fed during the observation, which means the scoring for this standard can be left blank. When the score for the observation is totaled, any blank standards in the Physical Care category can be counted as "yes" scores.

9. **Is each child who is preparing for sleep rocked, patted, or held by a caregiver?**

    Yes. Jeremy was sensitively prepared for sleep by his caregiver, Lia. She didn't put him in the crib abruptly upon noticing he was tired, but took a few minutes to rock and pat him. It wasn't necessary for Lia to wait until he was asleep before placing him in the crib.

10. **Is each child who is awake and ready to play removed from the crib promptly?**

    No. Benjamin's crying continued long enough that it became apparent that he was ready to get up. He should have been removed from the crib during the observation.

Interactions with Caregivers

11. **Is each caregiver responsive to the children's crying, gestures, or vocalizations?**

    No (one "yes"/one "no"). Mandy was observed diapering Kayla and feeding Katie, and she was consistently responsive to both babies' gestures and vocalizations, which led to a "yes" score for her. Although Lia was responsive to the babies in the play area during the first half of the observation, she became less responsive as time went on and became distracted by talking to the other caregiver. Specifically, she wasn't responsive because she ignored Benjamin's crying from the crib and didn't respond to Connor when he was vocalizing and gesturing.

12. **Is each caregiver frequently involved in positive interactions with the children?**

    No (one "yes"/one "no"). Mandy was scored a "yes" for this standard, as she interacted positively with both babies she cared for during the entire observation. Lia was scored a "no" because she wasn't consistently animated or playful with the babies in the play area. Although she was warm and responsive while putting Jeremy down for a nap, she didn't respond to him when he wanted different toys from the toy shelf. She also responded only occasionally to Connor in the infant seat, and she didn't talk to Katie while Katie played on the play mat.

13. **Does each caregiver stimulate the children's language by labeling objects, actions, or events?**

    No (one "yes"/one "no"). Mandy was scored a "yes" for this standard because she talked to the babies in a stimulating way by labeling objects and having simple conversations. Lia was scored a "no" because, although she talked to the babies a few times, her talking mainly involved managing the babies' behavior instead of stimulating their language development.

14. Does each caregiver encourage positive social interactions by helping children notice each other, use toys together, and touch one another gently?

Yes. Even though the caregivers didn't specifically encourage the babies to interact by talking about social skills, they both received "yes" scores because of more subtle actions. Lia positioned Connor so he could see one of the other playing babies. Mandy helped Kayla join Jeremy playing on the floor by handing her a similar toy and commenting on what Jeremy was doing.

15. Is each caregiver sensitive to the children's emotions and reactions?

No (one "yes"/one "no"). Mandy was scored a "yes" for this item because she responded sensitively to Kayla when she was interested in the mobile above the changing table and to Katie when she was excited about eating lunch. Lia was scored a "no" because she wasn't consistently sensitive to the babies' emotions and reactions while she was in the play area. Even though she was sensitive to Jeremy when he became sleepy, she ignored Benjamin's crying when he awoke, Connor's excitement when he saw a toy on the floor that he wanted, and Jeremy's desire to have some new toys from the shelf.

Total Score and Recommendations

Total score (number of "yes" scores) = 6, "Needs attention"

This classroom received a score that is less than 10, indicating that some aspects of the classroom need attention. Changes in some areas will make a big difference in the quality of care and classroom activities.

Although a low score on your first Quick Quality Check may concern you, remember that it is only one fifteen-minute observation. To get a complete picture of the quality of care provided to the children in the classroom, it is necessary to do several Quick Quality Checks on different days and at different times of day. One observation isn't enough to draw conclusions about the quality of care.

Once you have conducted several observations, you can examine patterns of scores within each category to identify areas where change is needed. The classroom in this example received four "no" scores in the Play category (standards 1, 3, 4, and 6), one "no" in Physical Care (standard 10), and four "no" scores in Interactions with Caregivers (standards 11, 12, 13, and 15).

Two situations occurred in this classroom that led to several of these "no" scores. One caregiver, Lia, didn't interact with the children in a consistently positive and responsive way, contributing to all the "no" scores. In addition, one baby remained in an infant seat for the entire observation and had no toys available, leading to "no" scores on standards 1, 3, and 4. By examining the reasons for "no" scores on each standard, you can identify topics for caregiver training or environmental change. (See page 31 for suggestions on meeting each standard.)

For the classroom in this example, removing infant seats from the play area and limiting their use to feeding would be a good first action. Also, if you were the director of this center, you might talk with the caregivers (either informally or in a staff meeting) about your expectations for responsive care, which include talking to babies, noticing their emotions and reactions, and responding to their crying and vocalizations.

After this training, continue to use Quick Quality Check to follow up on the suggestions you have made to caregivers and to identify other areas where quality may be improved.

Appendix 2: Toddler Quick Quality Check Example

The following scenario will help you learn to use Quick Quality Check in a toddler classroom. It describes activities and interactions that may be seen during Quick Quality Check observations. The scenarios are organized by category so you can practice scoring each quality standard. (For a description of how to score each standard, see page 25.)

Toddler Classroom Example

This toddler classroom accommodates children ages fifteen to thirty months old. Ten toddlers and two caregivers are present on the day of the observation. The first caregiver (Margaret) is changing one toddler's diaper while keeping an eye on another toddler (Austin) who is sitting on a potty-chair. The second caregiver (Theresa) is in the play area helping all the other children as they play with playdough.

Activities

1. **Do the children have opportunities to participate in teacher-involved activities or play?**

   Theresa is showing the children at the table how to roll out playdough and cut shapes with cookie cutters. She helps the children when they need more playdough and cookie cutters and tells them to put all of their cut-out shapes in the middle of the table for everyone to see.

   Yes_____ No_____

2. **Do the children have opportunities to participate in free play or independent activities?**

   The children continue to work with playdough at the table for about ten minutes. Then Margaret brings the children out of the bathroom area and says cheerfully, "Okay, everyone, it's story time. Everybody come sit in the circle!" Most of the children begin to put away their playdough and go to the circle area. Shay, however, refuses to put her playdough away when Theresa tells her to. Theresa says, "You need to come to the circle." Shay shakes her head and continues to cut shapes with the cookie cutters. Theresa begins to put the playdough away for her and takes the cookie cutters out of her hands. "You need to go sit in the circle now," she says firmly.

   Yes_____ No_____

3. **Does each child have opportunities to participate in social play and activities with other children?**

   While the children are playing with playdough, some of the older toddlers tell each other what shapes they are making. Twenty-month-old Kyle points to a cookie cutter that Kara has and says, "That!" Kara hands him the cookie cutter. Theresa notices this and thanks Kara for sharing nicely with Kyle. When Margaret calls all of the children over to the circle for story time, she says, "Everyone quiet now so we can hear the story. No talking during the story."
   Yes_____ No_____

4. **Does each child have opportunities for active physical play?**

   At the side of the classroom, there is a small slide and a rocking horse placed along the wall. During the observation, the children are involved in the playdough activity and story time and don't have time to play with these toys.
   Yes_____ No_____

5. **Does each child have opportunities to choose from several activities?**

   The children are involved in two activities during the observation—playing with playdough and story time. Children are not observed playing with the other toys in the classroom.
   Yes_____ No_____

Environment

6. **Do the children have access to manipulative materials?**

   The children are playing with small rolling pins and cookie cutters during the playdough activity. There are puzzles, shape-sorters, and waffle blocks on the shelves in the play area.
   Yes_____ No_____

7. **Do the children have access to dramatic play materials?**

   There is a play kitchen in the classroom with play food and dishes. There is also a box of dress-up clothes and a farm set with play people and animals.
   Yes_____ No_____

8. **Do the children have access to language materials?**

   While the children are playing with playdough, Theresa names the shapes the children are cutting out with the cookie cutters. Several times, she helps individual children say the names of the shapes. She also says the words "cookie cutter" and "rolling pin" to the younger toddlers as she hands out the materials. As story time begins, Margaret shows the children the book she is going to read, tells them the title, and begins to read out loud.
   Yes_____ No_____

9. **Do the children have access to a quiet, cozy, or private area for play or relaxation?**

   As story time begins, several of the children sit close to Margaret on the floor, forming a loose circle around her. Two of the toddlers go to sit in a nearby area; one sits in a bean bag chair and one lies on some big pillows. Margaret tells them they can sit there as long as they are quiet and listening to the story.
   Yes_____ No_____

10. **Do the children have an appropriate amount of space available to play or move about?**

    The classroom play space contains two round tables at one end, an open space in the middle, and a kitchen area, toy shelves, and the quiet/cozy area at the other end. All of the toys are put away during the observation.
    Yes_____ No_____

Interactions with Caregivers

11. **Is each caregiver frequently involved in positive interactions with children?**

    Theresa talks pleasantly to the children while they play with playdough, helping them name shapes and praising children when they share. She becomes frustrated when Shay doesn't want to put the playdough away, and says, "You need to go sit in the circle now," somewhat harshly. Margaret is heard saying nursery rhymes with the children while they are in the bathroom area and she says, "You went potty in the potty-chair! Great job!" to Austin. She then cheerfully asks the children to come to the circle area for story time, gently tells them to be quiet and listen, and cuddles with some of them on the floor as she begins to read.
    Yes_____ No_____

12. **Is each caregiver sensitive to the children's emotions and reactions?**

    Consider information from the scenarios already described.
    Yes_____ No_____

13. **Does each caregiver stimulate the children's language through activities and conversation?**

    Consider information from the scenarios already described.
    Yes_____ No_____

14. **Does each caregiver promote positive social development by helping children interact and cooperate?**

    Consider information from the scenarios already described.
    Yes_____ No_____

15. **Does each caregiver use positive guidance techniques such as redirection and positive reinforcement?**

When Shay isn't allowed to continue playing with playdough, she begins to cry. Theresa takes the playdough and cookie cutters from her, puts them away, and goes to sit in the circle with the others. Shay gets up from the table, lies down on the floor next to the circle area, and continues to cry quietly. Theresa ignores her.

Yes____ No____

Scoring

Play

1. **Do the children have opportunities to participate in teacher-involved activities or play?**

   Yes. Theresa was available in the play area and participated in the children's activity by helping them and talking with them. The two toddlers in the bathroom aren't considered for this standard because they weren't in the play area.

2. **Do the children have opportunities to participate in free play or independent activities?**

   No. The children were involved in whole-group activities throughout the observation. When Shay indicated that she would like to continue playing with playdough instead of going to story time, the caregiver insisted that she stop playing and join the group. During the observation, no children played independently.

3. **Does each child have opportunities to participate in social play and activities with other children?**

   Yes. Even though the children were asked not to talk during story time, they were allowed to interact during the time they played with playdough. Theresa didn't ask them to be quiet during this time, encouraged group interactions, and praised the children for sharing the materials.

4. **Does each child have opportunities for active physical play?**

   No. This classroom does contain toys for active physical play. However, the children were involved in group activities and weren't allowed to play with the slide or rocking horse during the observation.

5. **Does each child have opportunities to choose from several activities?**

   No. The children weren't allowed to choose their activities during the observation; they were required to participate in the playdough activity and the story time. In order to score this standard a "yes," the playdough and story time activities would have been available, but not required. In addition, children would have been allowed to play with some of the other classroom toys if they wanted to, making three activities available.

Environment

6. Do the children have access to manipulative materials?

No. Although there were more than two types of manipulative materials in the classroom, the children only had access to one type (playdough) during the observation. The children were not allowed to leave the playdough and story time activities to play with the other toys during the observation.

7. Do the children have access to dramatic play materials?

No. Although there were more than two types of dramatic play materials in the classroom, they were not available to the children during the observation.

8. Do the children have access to language materials?

No. Only one type of language material was available to the children during the observation. The playdough toys can be counted as a type of language material because the caregiver made a conscious effort to use the toys to teach the children words. Even though Margaret read the children a book, the children weren't able to touch or use the book themselves; therefore, this doesn't count as a language material available to children.

9. Do the children have access to a quiet, cozy, or private area for play or relaxation?

Yes. The bean bag chair and the pillows provided a cozy, quiet area, and the children were allowed to use them during the observation.

10. Do the children have an appropriate amount of space available to play or move about?

Yes. The play space was big enough to accommodate all of the children without crowding, and the space wasn't cluttered with toys and equipment during the observation.

Interactions with Caregivers

11. Is each caregiver frequently involved in positive interactions with children?

No (one "yes"/one "no"). Margaret received a "yes" score for this standard because all of her interactions with the children were warm, animated, and affectionate. She did require the children to come to the circle area and be quiet while listening to the story, but she didn't do it in a negative way. Theresa received a "no" score because she was observed in a negative interaction with Shay while trying to get her to put away the playdough. Even though she was involved in positive interactions with the children during the playdough activity, the one negative interaction caused her to receive a "no."

12. Is each caregiver sensitive to the children's emotions and reactions?

Yes. Both caregivers received "yes" scores for this standard because they were both observed being sensitive to the children's emotions and reactions more often than they were observed being insensitive. Theresa was not sensitive to Shay's emotions when she didn't want to put away the playdough, but all of Theresa's other interactions with the children were sensitive. Margaret acknowledged Austin's success with the potty-chair and allowed some of the children to sit in the cozy area during the reading time.

13. Does each caregiver stimulate the children's language through activities and conversation?

Yes. Margaret was scored a "yes" for this standard because she recited nursery rhymes with the children, talked to Austin about going potty, and read to the children during story time. Theresa was scored a "yes" because she used the playdough activity to teach the children new words by labeling the materials and asking them to name shapes.

14. Does each caregiver promote positive social development by helping children interact and cooperate?

No (one "yes"/one "no"). Theresa was scored a "yes" because she was actively and positively involved with the children in the group playdough activity, and she praised children when they shared the materials. Margaret encouraged a group activity, but she didn't use the activity to promote the children's social development because she didn't allow the children to talk or interact during the story. This led to a "no" score for her.

15. Does each caregiver use positive guidance techniques such as redirection and positive reinforcement?

No (one "yes"/one "no"). Theresa responded harshly when Shay didn't want to put the playdough away. Instead of explaining ("We're going to listen to a story now"), providing choices ("Where would you like to sit in the circle?"), or redirecting her ("Could you help me put all these cookie cutters in the box?"), she reprimanded her and pulled the toys out of her hands. Thus, she received a "no." Margaret was not observed being involved in any situation that required her to discipline the children. This led to a score of "yes" for her.

Total Score and Recommendations

Total score (number of "yes" scores) = 6, "Needs attention"

This classroom received a score of less than 10, indicating that some aspects of the classroom need attention. Changes in some areas will make a big difference in the quality of care and classroom activities.

Before taking any action, do several more Quick Quality Checks in the classroom, observing at different times of the day. A single fifteen-minute observation can't give a complete picture of the quality of care. If, after several observations, you find the scores are consistently low or particular standards are consistently not met, you will want to think about making some changes.

First, consider the scores within each category to see where standards are not met. For example, this classroom received three "no" scores in the Play category (standards 2, 4, and 5), three "no" scores in Environment (standards 6, 7, and 8), and three "no" scores in Interactions with Caregivers (standards 11, 14, and 15).

Second, examine the reasons for the "no" scores. In this example, all of the "no" scores in the Play and Environment categories were related to the fact that the children were required to participate in two large-group activities during the entire observation and weren't permitted to play with most of the toys or participate in free play. Thus, one change—having more than one activity available rather than requiring children to participate in a single activity—would make a big difference.

In interactions with caregivers, each of the two caregivers contributed to the "no" scores. If these same standards were scored "no" across several observations, it would be useful to discuss with the caregivers the importance of positive interactions between teachers and children *and* among children. Analyzing the pattern of scores helps target the aspects of the classroom that need attention. (See page 35 for suggestions on meeting each standard.)

In this classroom, for example, two steps can be taken to improve the quality of children's experiences. First, talk with the caregivers about arranging a daily schedule that ensures a variety of toys is available to the children all the time. Second, eliminate required participation in group activities. After taking these steps, continue to use Quick Quality Check to follow up on the suggestions you have made to caregivers and to identify other areas where quality may be improved.

Appendix 3: Information for Classroom Staff about the Quick Quality Check Observation

This appendix contains two handouts that can be used to introduce Quick Quality Check to classroom staff. Each gives a brief general overview of Quick Quality Check and then describes the categories of care covered in a Quick Quality Check observation. The first handout covers the Infant categories, and the second reviews the Toddler categories. We recommend that directors photocopy the handouts and pass them out to classroom staff when introducing the Quick Quality Check. The handouts make it easy to discuss each part of the Quick Quality Check and be sure that staff members recognize the importance of each item in providing quality care.

The Quick Quality Check for Infants

Quick Quality Check is a tool for child care center administrators to use in looking at the quality of learning activities and care taking place in infant and toddler classrooms. Your center director will periodically use Quick Quality Check to observe in your classroom, and she or he will note whether certain classroom activities are occurring. Here are the three categories of care in Quick Quality Check for infants and examples of what the director will be looking for.

Infants

Play

The Play category includes the toys and space available to the children; the use of infant seats, swings, and playpens; and the children's opportunities to practice motor skills and to interact with caregivers and other children.

Quality care includes

- a variety of toys available to all of the babies in the play area;
- a play area that is not crowded or cluttered with toys;
- only brief and occasional use of infant seats and swings when children are awake and not eating;
- opportunities for babies to play with toys and practice motor skills;
- opportunities for babies to play with caregivers and with other babies.

Physical Care

Physical Care encompasses interactions and procedures involved in diapering, feeding, and napping routines.

Quality care includes

- caregivers who speak and respond warmly to babies who are being fed and diapered;
- babies who are held by a caregiver during bottle-feeding;
- caregivers who prepare babies for sleep by rocking, patting, or holding;
- babies who are removed from their cribs when they are awake and ready to play.

Interactions with Caregivers

Interactions with Caregivers includes the responsiveness of caregivers to the children and the caregivers' involvement in the children's development of language and social skills.

Quality care includes

- caregivers who are responsive to the babies' crying, vocalizations, emotions, and reactions;
- warm, playful, and affectionate interactions between caregivers and babies;
- caregivers who talk to the babies to stimulate their language development;
- caregivers who help babies notice each other, touch each other gently, and begin to use toys together.

The Quick Quality Check for Toddlers

Quick Quality Check is a tool for child care center administrators to use in looking at the quality of learning activities and care taking place in infant and toddler classrooms. Your center director will periodically use Quick Quality Check to observe in your classroom, and she or he will note whether certain classroom activities are occurring. Here are the three categories of care in Quick Quality Check for toddlers and examples of what the director will be looking for.

Toddlers

Activities

The Activities category includes the opportunities children have for different types of activities, including play with caregivers, independent play, social play, and physically active play.

Quality care includes

- ◆ a caregiver available to play with children in the play area;
- ◆ time available for children's free play and social play with other children;
- ◆ active physical play toys available in the classroom;
- ◆ different activities available for children to choose from.

Environment

The Environment category includes the availability to the children of different types of toys, ample space, and quiet areas.

Quality care includes

- ◆ several types of toys available to the children, including building toys, pretend-play toys, and books;
- ◆ a quiet, private place in the classroom available to the children;
- ◆ a play space that is big enough for the children and not crowded with furniture and toys.

Interactions with Caregivers

Interactions with Caregivers includes the responsiveness of caregivers to the children, the promotion of language development and social skills, and the use of positive guidance techniques.

Quality care includes

- ◆ caregivers who are involved in positive play and talk with the children;
- ◆ caregivers who are sensitive to the children's emotions;
- ◆ caregivers who are involved in teaching the children language and social skills;
- ◆ positive guidance, such as redirecting children and noticing their good behavior.

Appendix 4: What the Research Says about Quality Child Care

Quick Quality Check Validity

Several methods were used to show that overall scores that Quick Quality Check produces provide accurate and meaningful information on classroom quality and that each of the Quick Quality Check standards is an important component of these scores. Feedback from child care center directors also was incorporated into the final version of the instrument.

A 1997 study established the criteria used to determine the validity and reliability of Quick Quality Check in assessing the quality of infant and toddler programs. Twelve child care center directors completed a total of seventy-seven Quick Quality Check observations. In addition, observations were done in the same classrooms using both Quick Quality Check and condensed versions of two well-known rating methods, the Infant/Toddler Environment Rating Scale (Harms, Cryer, and Clifford 1990) and the Assessment Profile for Early Childhood Programs (Abbott-Shim and Sibley 1987).

The Quick Quality Check observations produced scores similar to the other rating methods and produced similar rankings of high, mediocre, and poor quality among the classrooms. The quality rankings that Quick Quality Check produced also were similar to findings of other recent studies of child care quality.

The validity of the Quick Quality Check content was determined by cross-referencing each Quick Quality Check standard with results of current research. This cross-referencing was part of a comprehensive review of the child care literature that occurred during the development of Quick Quality Check (see tables 1 and 2, starting on page 60). Seven of the standards have not been specifically examined but are supported by the National Association for the Education of Young Children and are included in the Child Development Associate competency standards. In addition, these seven standards are indirectly supported by research, and they are included in other observational instruments such as the Observational Ratings of the Caregiving Environment (NICHD 1996, 2000a), the Infant/Toddler Environment Rating Scale (Harms, Cryer, and Clifford 1990), and the Assessment Profile for Early Childhood Programs (Abbott-Shim and Sibley 1987).

Furthermore, the validity of the standards was established during a review of Quick Quality Check by the twelve directors who participated in the validity study. The directors completed a questionnaire on their satisfaction with and opinions about Quick Quality Check. The directors rated six possible uses for Quick Quality Check as either very helpful or somewhat helpful. In rating the importance of each Quick Quality Check standard, the directors rated all thirty standards as either very important or somewhat important.

The Research Behind the Quick Quality Check Standards

Each standard in Quick Quality Check for Infants and Quick Quality Check for Toddlers is important to children's development and the process of providing quality care. On the tables that follow are references to research articles and professional books that address each standard and a brief statement concerning their findings. The statements summarize recent research information on the importance of each standard to children's development.

Table 1. References for Quick Quality Check Infant Standards

Quick Quality Check Standard	Reference	Finding
1. Variety of toys	NICHD, 1996, 2000a	The frequency and quality of positive caregiving is higher when the physical environment is safe, clean, and stimulating.
	Burchinal et al., 1996	Opportunities for infants to play with a variety of objects is necessary to enhance cognitive development.
	Bolig et al., 1991	Without adequate equipment, children become frustrated and angry or passive and withdrawn.
	Cryer and Phillipsen, 1997	Sufficient toys and materials are often missing in the average infant/toddler room.
2. Amount of space	Trancik and Evans, 1995	Child care center environments should have ample space for movement in order to promote exploration.
	Scarr, Eisenberg, and Deater-Deckard, 1994	Aspects of care that are regulated (such as space) are shown to be related to other aspects of quality care (such as positive interactions).
3. Removed from swings or seats	No specific data	See references for standards 1 and 5.
4. Motor skills experience	No specific data	See references for standards 1 and 2.
5. Interactions with other children	Cryer and Phillipsen, 1997	On average, infant rooms score between "minimal" and "good" for the peer interaction item on the Infant/Toddler Environment Rating Scale (ITERS). Caregivers were not seen pointing out or reinforcing positive social interactions.
	Clarke-Stewart, 1993	Playing with different children in child care is related to more advanced intellectual and social abilities.

Quick Quality Check Standard	Reference	Finding
6. Interactions with caregivers	Clarke-Stewart, 1993	When caregivers act as facilitators by responding to interests and goals, children are more independent, cooperative, and social.
	Bolig et al., 1991	Without adults to supervise and provide new ideas for play, children often become frightened, unfocused, and aggressive.
7. Responsiveness during feeding and diapering	No specific data	Included in the ITERS. See references for standards 1, 2, and 5.
8. Held during feeding	No specific data	Included in the ITERS.
9. Prepared for sleep	No specific data	Included in the ITERS.
10. Removed from crib	Bolig et al., 1991	Physical abuse includes infants being left in cribs for extended periods. Also see references for standards 1 and 5.
11. Responsive to crying and vocalizations	NICHD, 2000b	The amount of language directed at children in child care is related to their development of cognitive and language skills. Child care with a high degree of positive caregiver-child interactions can lead to better mother-child interactions.
12. Frequency of positive interactions	No specific data	See references for standards 6, 11, and 15.
13. Stimulation of language	Burchinal et al., 1996	Caregivers who take turns in interactions and share periods of joint focus with infants facilitate language development. Higher quality care as measured by the ITERS is related to better receptive language and communication skills development.
	NICHD, 2000b	How often caregivers speak to children, ask them questions, and respond to their vocalizations is positively related to children's language abilities at fifteen, twenty-four, and thirty-six months of age, and to school readiness at age three.
14. Encouragement of social interactions	No specific data	See references for standard 5.
15. Sensitive to emotions and reactions	NICHD, 1996, 2000a	Quality care, as defined through caregiver interactive behavior, best predicts children's development.
	Cryer and Phillipsen, 1997	The average infant/toddler room scores between "minimal" and "good" on caregiver-child interaction on the ITERS. Sensitivity to feelings, reactions, and individual needs is rarely seen.

Table 2. References for Quick Quality Check Toddler Standards

Quick Quality Check Standard	Reference	Finding
1. Teacher-involved activities	Clarke-Stewart, 1993	When caregivers act as facilitators by responding to interests and goals, children are more independent, cooperative, and social.
	Hestenes, Kontos, and Bryan, 1993	Children display more positive affect and less-intense negative affect when caregivers are more highly engaged in their activities.
2. Free play/independent activities	Trancik and Evans, 1995	Having control of environmental resources leads to children's feelings of accomplishment and independence, whereas a lack of control may result in feelings of helplessness.
	Clarke-Stewart, 1993	In highly controlled classrooms, children show less cooperation, less initiative, and less imaginative play than children in less controlled classrooms.
3. Social play/activities	Clarke-Stewart, 1993	In less controlled classrooms, children show more imaginative play, work, and helping with peers.
	Bolig et al., 1991	Forming peer relationships is essential to normal development and the lack of opportunities or encouragement to do so is a type of neglect.
4. Active physical play	No specific data	See references for infant standard 1. Included in ITERS and Assessment Profile (Abbott-Shim and Sibley 1987).
5. Choice of activities	Clarke-Stewart, 1993	In highly controlled classrooms, children show less cooperation, less initiative, and less imaginative play than children in less controlled classrooms.
	Trancik and Evans, 1995	Having control of environmental resources leads to children's feelings of accomplishment and independence, whereas a lack of control may result in feelings of helplessness.
6. Manipulative materials	No specific data	See references for infant standard 1.
7. Dramatic play materials	Howes and Matheson, 1992	Children's social-pretend play is linked to emotional, cognitive, linguistic, and social development.
	Cryer and Phillipsen, 1997	The materials for pretend play are often missing or inaccessible in the average infant/toddler room.

Quick Quality Check Standard	Reference	Finding
8. Language materials	NICHD, 2000b	Language stimulation in the child care setting is related to children's better performance on cognitive and language assessments at fifteen, twenty-four, and thirty-six months of age.
	Dunn, Beach, and Kontos, 1994	Having materials available to children, displaying functional and environmental print, interactive book reading, and providing materials that promote literacy in play settings have all been shown to enhance the development of literacy and language.
	Cryer and Phillipsen, 1997	Books and pictures are often missing or inaccessible in the average infant/toddler room.
	Herb and Willoughby-Herb, 1985	Providing infants and toddlers with books to manipulate and choose from independently promotes activities that enhance language and promotes early reading and writing.
9. Quiet, cozy, private area	Trancik and Evans, 1995	Having a choice between public and private spaces is important in the development of competency and provides for uninterrupted play, concentration, and observation.
	Zeegers, Readdick, and Hansen-Gandy, 1994	Child care children need time for quiet, private play for healthy, autonomous development. Younger children have expanded needs for privacy. The availability of rest spaces helps children learn to regulate their feelings of fatigue.
10. Amount of space	Trancik and Evans, 1995	Child care environments should have ample space for movement in order to promote exploration.
11. Frequency of positive interactions	Zaslow, 1991	Quality care that includes positive caregiver-child interactions best predicts children's optimal development.
12. Sensitive to emotions and reactions	NICHD, 1996, 2000a	Quality care, as defined through caregiver interactive behavior, best predicts children's development.
	Cryer and Phillipsen, 1997	The average infant/toddler room scores between "minimal" and "good" on caregiver-child interaction on the ITERS. Sensitivity to feelings, reactions, and individual needs is rarely seen.
13. Language stimulation	NICHD, 2000b	How often caregivers speak to children, ask them questions, and respond to their vocalizations is positively related to children's language abilities at fifteen, twenty-four, and thirty-six months of age, and to school readiness at age three.

Quick Quality Check Standard	Reference	Finding
14. Encouragement of social interactions	Clarke-Stewart, 1993	Playing with different children in child care is related to more advanced intellectual and social abilities.
15. Positive guidance	Bolig et al., 1991	Punishment is inappropriate when unaccompanied by verbal explanation or acceptable alternatives for behavior. Continued use of negative direction can interfere with the development of positive self-esteem.
	Weiss et al., 1992	Harsh discipline and aggression in children are consistently related.
	Reid, O'Leary, and Wolff, 1994	Distraction, when preceded by a reprimand, is effective in maintaining low rates of misbehavior in toddlers.
	Grusec and Goodnow, 1994	Techniques such as praise and withdrawal of attention help children internalize values more effectively than removal of privileges and physical punishment.

References for Table 1 and Table 2

The references listed here pertain only to Tables 1 and 2. For a complete list of references for the Quick Quality Check, please see the main reference list in appendix 5.

Abbott-Shim, M., and A. Sibley. 1987. *Assessment profile for early childhood programs*. Atlanta: Quality Assistance Co.

Bolig, R., R. Kantor-Martin, H. L. Nissen, and K. A. Volton. 1991. Contexts for maltreatment in daycare centers: Conceptualization and implications. *Children's Environments* 8:17–24.

Burchinal, M. R., J. E. Roberts, L. A. Nabors, and D. M. Bryant. 1996. Quality of center child care and infant cognitive and language development. *Child Development* 67:606–20.

Clarke-Stewart, A. 1993. *Daycare*. Cambridge, Mass.: Harvard University Press.

Cryer, D., and L. Phillipsen. 1997. A close-up look at child care program strengths and weaknesses. *Young Children* 52:51–65.

Dunn, L., S. A. Beach, and S. Kontos. 1994. Quality of the literacy environment in day care and children's development. *Journal of Research in Childhood Education* 9:24–33.

Grusec, J. E., and J. J. Goodnow. 1994. Impact of parental discipline methods on the child's internalization of values: A reconceptualization of current points of view. *Developmental Psychology* 30:4–19.

Harms, T., D. Cryer, and R. Clifford. 1990. *Infant/toddler environment rating scale*. New York: Teachers College.

Herb, S., and S. Willoughby-Herb. 1985. Books as toys. *Topics in Early Childhood Special Education* 5:83–92.

Hestenes, L. L., S. Kontos, and Y. Bryan. 1993. Children's emotional expression in child care centers varying in quality. *Early Childhood Research Quarterly* 8:295–307.

Howes, C., and C. C. Matheson. 1992. Sequences of development of competent play with peers: Social and social pretend play. *Developmental Psychology* 28:961–74.

National Institute of Child Health and Human Development (NICHD) Early Child Care Research Network. 1996. Characteristics of infant child care: Factors contributing to positive caregiving. *Early Childhood Research Quarterly* 11:269–306.

———. 2000a. Characteristics and quality of child care for toddlers and preschoolers. *Applied Developmental Science* 4:116–35.

———. 2000b. The relation of child care to cognitive and language development. *Child Development* 71:960–80.

Reid, M. J., S. G. O'Leary, and L. S. Wolff. 1994. Effects of maternal distraction and reprimands on toddlers' transgression and negative affect. *Journal of Abnormal Child Psychology* 22:237–45.

Scarr, S., M. Eisenberg, and K. Deater-Deckard. 1994. Measurement of quality in child care centers. *Early Childhood Research Quarterly* 9:131–51.

Trancik, A. M., and G. W. Evans. 1995. Spaces fit for children: Competency in the design of daycare center environments. *Children's Environments* 12:311–19.

Weiss, B., K. A. Dodge, J. E. Bates, and G. S. Petit. 1992. Some consequences of early harsh discipline: Child aggression and a maladaptive social information processing style. *Child Development* 63:1321–35.

Zaslow, M. J. 1991. Variation in child care quality and its implications for children. *Journal of Social Issues* 47:125–38.

Zeegers, S. K., C. A. Readdick, and S. Hansen-Gandy. 1994. Daycare children's establishment of territory to experience privacy. *Children's Environments* 11:265–71.

Appendix 5: References

Abbott-Shim, M., and A. Sibley. 1987. *Assessment profile for early childhood programs*. Atlanta: Quality Assistance Inc.

Bredekamp, S., and C. Copple, eds. 1997. *Developmentally appropriate practice in early childhood programs*. Washington, D.C.: National Association for the Education of Young Children.

Hart, B. M., and T. R. Risley. 1995. *Meaningful differences in the everyday experience of young American children*. Baltimore: Paul H. Brookes.

Harms, T., D. Cryer, and R. Clifford. 1990. *Infant/toddler environment rating scale*. New York: Teachers College.

Helburn, S., M. L. Culkin, J. Morris, N. Mocan, C. Howes, L. Phillilpsen, D. Bryant, R. Clifford, D. Cryer, E. Peisner-Feinberg, M. Burchinal, S. L. Kagan, and J. Rustici. 1995. *Cost, quality, and outcomes in child care centers*. Denver: Economics Department, Univ. of Colorado at Denver.

Herrera, E. 2000. The relationship between attribution, job satisfaction, and burnout in childcare settings. Unpublished master's thesis, Univ. of Kansas, Lawrence, Kansas.

Kisker, E. E., S. L. Hofferth, D. A. Phillips, and E. Farquhar. 1991. *A profile of child care settings: Early education and care in 1990* (Final report for U.S. Department of Education, Rep. No. LC88090001). Princeton: Mathematica.

Knoll, M. (1998). Validation of the Quick Check: An instrument designed for daycare center directors. Unpublished master's thesis, Univ. of Kansas, Lawrence, Kansas.

National Institute of Child Health and Human Development (NICHD). Early Child Care Research Network. 1996. Characteristics of infant child care: Factors contributing to positive caregiving. *Early Childhood Research Quarterly* 11:269–306.

———. 1999. Child outcomes when child-care center classes meet recommended standards for quality. *American Journal of Public Health* 89:1072–77.

———. 2000. Characteristics and quality of child care for toddlers and preschoolers. *Applied Developmental Science* 4:116–35.

Wilson, L. C., L. Douville-Watson, and M. A. Watson. 1995. *Infants and toddlers: Curriculum and teaching.* Albany: Delmar.

Other Resources from Redleaf Press

Infant and Toddler Experiences
by Fran Hast and Ann Hollyfield
Filled with experiences—not activities—that promote the healthiest development in infants and toddlers.

More Infant and Toddler Experiences
by Fran Hast and Ann Hollyfield
More quality developmental experiences for infants and toddlers in your care.

Beginning with Babies
by Mary Lou Kinney and Patricia Witt Ahrens
An easy-to-use guide containing dozens of activities to help teachers provide developmentally appropriate care for children from birth through fifteen months.

Prime Times: A Handbook for Excellence in Infant and Toddler Programs
by Jim Greenman and Anne Stonehouse
An essential guide to establishing a high-quality program for infant and toddler care.

The Art of Awareness: How Observation Can Transform Your Teaching
by Deb Curtis and Margie Carter
Do more than watch children—*be* with children. Covering different aspects of children's lives and how to observe them, as well as tips for gathering and preparing documentation, *The Art of Awareness* is an inspiring look at how to see the children in your care—and how to see what they see.

Transition Magician: Strategies for Guiding Young Children in Early Childhood Programs
by Nola Larson, Mary Henthorne, and Barbara Plum
More than 200 original learning activities will help teachers smoothly weave everyday activities together.

Transition Magician 2: More Strategies for Guiding Young Children in Early Childhood Programs
by Mary Henthorne, Nola Larson, and Ruth Chvojicek
Picking up where the first *Transition Magician* left off, *Transition Magician 2* contains simple tools to help evaluate environments and schedules and to prevent problems by planning transitions. Contains over 200 new learning activities perfect for any transition time in the classroom.

Transition Magician for Families: Helping Parents and Children with Everyday Routines
by Ruth Chvojicek, Mary Henthorne, and Nola Larson
Dozens of activity ideas for caregivers to share with families to simplify the everyday transitions outside of child care.

Call toll-free 800-423-8309
www.redleafpress.org